Published in the United Kingdom by Krystal C King.

Content Copyright © 2019 by Krystal C King.

Illustrations (except where attributed) are copyright © 2019 by Krystal C King.

Reproduction and distribution of copyright illustrations made by the author, must be referenced correctly, and subject to fair usage.

This book or any portion thereof, may not be wholly reproduced or used in a commercial manner without the written permission of the publisher and author.

The contents of this book, may be used only with good intention and responsibility. The contents of this book may therefore be used for educational and teaching purposes.

Details of this book have been sent to the British Library via the Nielsen Database.

Published with Blurb Books at blurb.co.uk.

Page intentionally left blank

PREFACE

"Judge not a tree by the size of its seed, and the length of its growth."

I realised that on my spiritual journey, certain things happen for a particular reason. Similar experiences may keep recurring in one's life, for one to focus and learn a specific lesson.

I have realised that on one's spiritual journey, there can be many different interpretations of the same concept, not all of which will necessarily apply to oneself, or others, at a particular moment in time. I have realised that some questions, if remain unanswered, are best left to be answered by one's self.

In that way, by searching inwardly for the solution, one gets an in-depth appreciation of not only one's self, but also of the corresponding external world that is *relevant* to oneself and one's situation. This then allows one to mature in a way that is unique to one's situation, so that one can influence and motivate others like oneself.

This book answers a conglomeration of celestial and mystical questions arisen from reflecting on the concept of a Mustard seed. These questions arose during a phase in life where one arrived at a challenging cross road in life. This book, thus serves as a workbook for the mind.

I dedicate this book to myself, and to my dearest family and friends; especially those who have stood by me during its making. I dedicate this book also to those on this plane and beyond, who have directly or indirectly resulted in its creation, to our Angels and Spirit Guides, and to the Divine Infinite.

Finally, I dedicate this book to **You**.

"You shall know them by the fruits they bear".
 - (Matthew 7:16)

Page intentionally left blank

CONTENTS

SECTION ONE

CHAPTER 1
- Mustard Seeds

CHAPTER 2
- Nourishment

CHAPTER 3
- Repetition and Growth

SECTION TWO

CHAPTER 4
- Branches of Energy

CHAPTER 5
- Fruits of the Tree

CHAPTER 6
-Dreams

CHAPTER 7
- Celestial Mirrors

CONTENTS

SECTION THREE

INDEX: Celestial Atlas

SECTION FOUR

References

Attributes

Closing statements

"The Kingdom of Heaven is like a grain of mustard seed, that when it is grown, it is greater than all the herbs and becomes a tree."

- Matthew 13: 31-32

CHAPTER ONE
MUSTARD SEEDS

A young lady once had a dream about buying a whole basket of mustard seeds. Even the sales clerk was shocked that she would pick such small seeds. Said the sales clerk - "Oh how strange, people do not often choose those seeds anymore."

What is the significance of a mustard seed?

The mustard seed is one of the smallest seeds in our world today. The size of the seed ranges from only 1 to 2 millimetres.

Mustard has been one of the most widely grown and used spices in the world for many centuries.

The mustard seed is thought to have originated in Ancient Egypt, and has been used by many cultures in medicine, and as a spice across the ages, and to this date.

Seeds are often the precursor to which life sprouts from, or to which an idea is planted, like a seed into the mind. From this, a revelation, or independent thought, or idea often arises.

Seeds are like parables told across the ages, maturing into trees of knowledge and wisdom as they grow and branch in the minds of individuals, and subsequently communities.

The mustard seed is also like a lone individual who is not afraid to venture outside the box, and outside the norms of society, just because they are different. It is often here, where the deepest and most revolutionary ideas are sought. This is one of the things that makes such an individual unique.

"*Wisdom* is the principle thing; therefore get wisdom: and with all thy getting, *get understanding*".
- Proverbs (of Solomon) 4: 7

"The kingdom of heaven is like a mustard seed, which a man took and sowed in his field, which indeed is the least of all the seeds; but when it is grown it is greater than the herbs and becomes a tree, so that the birds of the air come and nest in its branches."
- (Matt. 13:31-32)

What does all of this mean?

Parables have many meanings and can be applied to many different situations. Parables are beautiful, versatile and unique. This is because they can have many meanings to their illustrations, and thereby in so doing, stretch the mind by making one utilise one's imagination, and encourage one to think outside the normal constraints of thought.

This parable is unique in the sense that it highlights, that one has control over one's situations and destiny. You are your creator, in a sense. If one can move a mountain with the faith of mustard seed, think what one could do if one unlocked one's full potential.

Raboni Yeshua (also know as Jesus), Hebraic Master Teacher, taught that **we are to do greater things even than Him (John 14:12); and that the Kingdom of God, and the Spirit of God, are all within us.**

Therefore the ability to create is within us also. However, we are to use these lessons with great wisdom, as with knowledge also comes great responsibility.

Concepts and teachings such as these, have no doubt been around throughout the ages; and would have been referred to by different names within different religious systems, region, or time period. However, essentially, for the greatest appreciation, one would benefit from developing an understanding, that it is not the name of the concept or teaching that is the most important, but rather the message that it holds, and the best way of delivering said message.

Throughout life, I have come to realise that **the imagination is one of the strongest gifts that one possesses.** When expanded, the imagination can make the seemingly impossible, **possible.**

If you look around you, every single item you have, began with a thought in someone's mind. This is from the pen you write with, to the shoes on your feet. Even Creation itself, began with a thought, before God ("The Elohim") spoke, and made creation as we know it, into existence.

Another example right in front of you, is this book. This book began with a single thought. After that thought, I then wrote down the words I wanted to say to you, and how I wanted to deliver the information. At the end of this process, I then executed those actions, which has manifested as the words you are now reading.

I imagined it all, before it came to be, and then it simply was. At first, I did not think that I had the time or the scope to achieve to completion this project. However with hard work, motivation and faith in myself, (faith even as tiny as a mustard seed), the fruit from that seed of thought then began to grow.

I encourage you to apply these concepts and principles to various areas of your life to reap positive benefits.

REMEMBER THESE <u>FOUR</u> KEYS:

1. **Be comfortable with starting small.**
2. **Be comfortable with being different.**
3. **Keep your focus fixed on your goal.**
4. **Then, take a leap of faith,** even, if it just a small one.

The righteous shall live
by faith'
- (Habakkuk 2:4)

How can we apply this to our personal lives?

The grain of mustard seed is also like man before he becomes spiritually mature. They are in a state of growth and regeneration. When he or she gains knowledge and wisdom through the experience of life's lessons, they then mature into a tree.

Now, truths and understanding, have branches in which to nest. These nests of knowledge can now be shared, to fertilise and nourish other seeds (individuals whom one teaches, inspires and thereby enlightens).

There are <u>THREE</u> concepts to understand in applying this knowledge:

1. THERE IS ALWAYS ROOM FOR CONTINUAL GROWTH AND DEVELOPMENT.

This will be needed in different aspects of one's life to another persons life. Only our Cosmic Creator is perfect, as He is "The ALL". "He" is the essence of everything and everyone around us. Humans have been gifted with the choice to be able to seek knowledge and learn. This allows us to develop and finesse our skills in order to provide meaningful contributions towards our own lives, and in those around us. We also have the choice to do this in whatever environment suits us best.

2. THERE IS ALWAYS NEED FOR NOURISHMENT

Humans are like plants, because, we will always need nourishment to continue to grow. Take for example, a house plant. At some point, the nutrients in the plant's soil will become exhausted, and will need replacing. The nutrients needed will also vary depending on the plant, and sometimes its phase of growth. This is just like a human, because at various stages in life, some of us will need different supplies of nutrients than others to continue to mature healthily. These nutrients come in different forms, ranging from physical nutrients, to things such as the experiences we have ourselves; and also the experiences we take part in and guide others through.

"Man shall not live on bread alone, but on every word that comes from the mouth of God." (Matthew 4:4)

3. FULLY MATURED FRUIT REAP THE BEST SEEDS

No one said it was going to be easy! For some, life's journey will be much more intense than others. This is because we have each incarnated into this life, with different lessons to learn and master. When things go presumedly "wrong" in your life, sometimes, depending on what those things are, they are simply a way of the "Universe" or "God", giving you the nourishment that your soul needs so that you can continue to grow.

Sometimes it is nourishment to become stronger, so that in turn, you can help others to grow. Only once you are strong enough, and have the correct knowledge and experience, can you then share this wisdom to others, in a way which they can understand and use.

For example, this book is a cultivation of various seeds (of knowledge) that I have gathered along the way. It is a cultivation of taking a leap of faith to create something I thought was beyond my capabilities, reach, and understanding.

I have completed it through hard work, faith and determination. My faith brought with it, the spiritual guidance needed to walk and endure the path to see through to its completion.

From reading this book, you will be then be set to become a more fruitful tree, and help to cultivate more fruitful trees of your own.

" ... Truly I tell you, if you have faith as small as a mustard seed, you can say to this mountain: 'Move from here to there,' and it will move. Nothing will be impossible for you."
– (Matthew 17:20)

CHAPTER 2
NOURISHMENT

"Through the middle of the street of the city; also, on either side of the river, the tree of life with its twelve kinds of fruit, yielding its fruit each month. The leaves of the tree were for the healing of the nations."
- (Rev. 22:2)

What are the Tree of Life and the Sephirot ?

What are they & how do they relate to life?

I would not claim to be an adept expert on the Trees of Life and Knowledge.

However, like everything in life, things also derive meaning dependant on how **you** analyse, and apply them.

There are many depictions of the "Tree of Life" across many religious systems.

However, the Judeo-Christian teachings of "The Tree of Life", in its mystical sense traces back to the "Sephirot". These are the **ten emanations,** divine life-force channels, or attributes, studied in the **Sciences of the Kabbalah (Wisdom of the Torah)**; through which the **Divine Infinite ("Ein Sof")** reveals itself, through a metaphysical system. This leads to what we in turn experience as reality. ("Kabbalah", means *"to receive"*).

In addition, the Judeo-Christian doctrines also describe a great judgement in the Book of Revelation. The Day of Judgement is depicted in many religious systems, even tracing back to Ancient Egypt. Metatron in Judeo-Christian doctrine is the "Archangel of Judgement", the "Highest Ranking Angel" and "Celestial Scribe". Like many others, his name also carries many other meanings, all of which exceed the objectives of this book. Metatron, in some Kabbalistic texts, also refers to the concept of Enoch after *his whole body ascended into Heaven.* The Sephirot can also be overlayed onto the cube of Metatron.

"And Enoch walked with God; and he was not; for God took him". - (Gen 5:24)

Each aspect of the Sephirot Tree, corresponds to various conscious emotional, intellectual, and superconscious phenomena. These are reflected off of each other on the physical and spiritual realms alike.

These also correspond to the left, middle, and right axes of the Sephirot Tree.

CATEGORY	LEFT AXIS - Female Aspect	MIDDLE AXIS - Female/ Male	RIGHT AXIS - Male Aspect
Intellect	2: Binah - (Understanding)	3: Da'at - (Knowledge)	1: Chokhmah - (Wisdom)
Emotions	5: Gevurah - (Discipline)	6: Tiferet - (Beauty)	4: Chesed - (Kindness)
	8: Hod - (Glory)	9: Yesod - (Foundation)	7: Netzach - (Eternity)
		10: *Malkuth - (Kingship)	

Table: Axes of the Sephirot Tree

Within the "consciousness" of the Sephirot Tree, there are 10 levels, with 22 connecting paths; and three vertical axes, as mentioned above. The ten Sephirot, also directly correspond to the four hebrew letter configuration of "God's Divine Name", " יהוה " (or "**YHWH**"in Latin transcript).

This is also referred to as the **Tetragrammaton. "YHWH"** was the Biblical God of the Kingdom of Israel, but was then later worshipped as the Infinite "Creator God" after the 6th Century BCE. There are many levels to the meaning of " יהוה ".

Summatively, the **10 Sephirot**, **22 paths**, with its **3 axes** amount to what is described as **" 32 Paths of Wisdom"**.

These systems are also linked to the Elementary, Planetary, and Zodiac Systems. See Illustrations 1-3, for such examples.

There are **"Four Worlds"** within the Sephirot System, which correspond to "**Four Planes of Existence**. These worlds, or planes, also correspond to various elements.

LETTER OF יהוה	WORLD	TYPE OF WORLD	TYPE OF PLANE	KETHER	MEANING	ELEMENT
Yod (י)	1	Archetypal World (Atziluth)	Plane of Will/Spirit	Chockmah	Revelation, Superconsciousness. Supreme Wisdom of the ALL.	
He (ה)	2	Creative World (Briah)	Mental Plane	Binah	Intellectual understanding. Self awareness	
Waw (ו)	3	Formative World (Yetzirah)	Emotional Plane	Sefirots: Chesed, Gevurah, Tiferet, Netzach, Hod, Yesod	The drive to create form. The numerical value of "Waw" is also 6.	
He (ה)	4	Physical world (Assiah)	Material Plane	Malchut	To bring into existence. "To receive."	

Table: The Four Worlds of the Sephirot

After pondering for a long time on the Tree of Life, I subsequently realised, that if God is within us, and we are meant to be like God; then if we truly understand the three axes of the Sephirot and all its tiers, then we realise that they all lie within us also.

The 10 tiers also correspond to "Fruits of the Spirit". Everything that is reflected inwards, is ultimately reflected outwards.

"As above, so below. As within, so without"
"As the Universe, so the Soul."

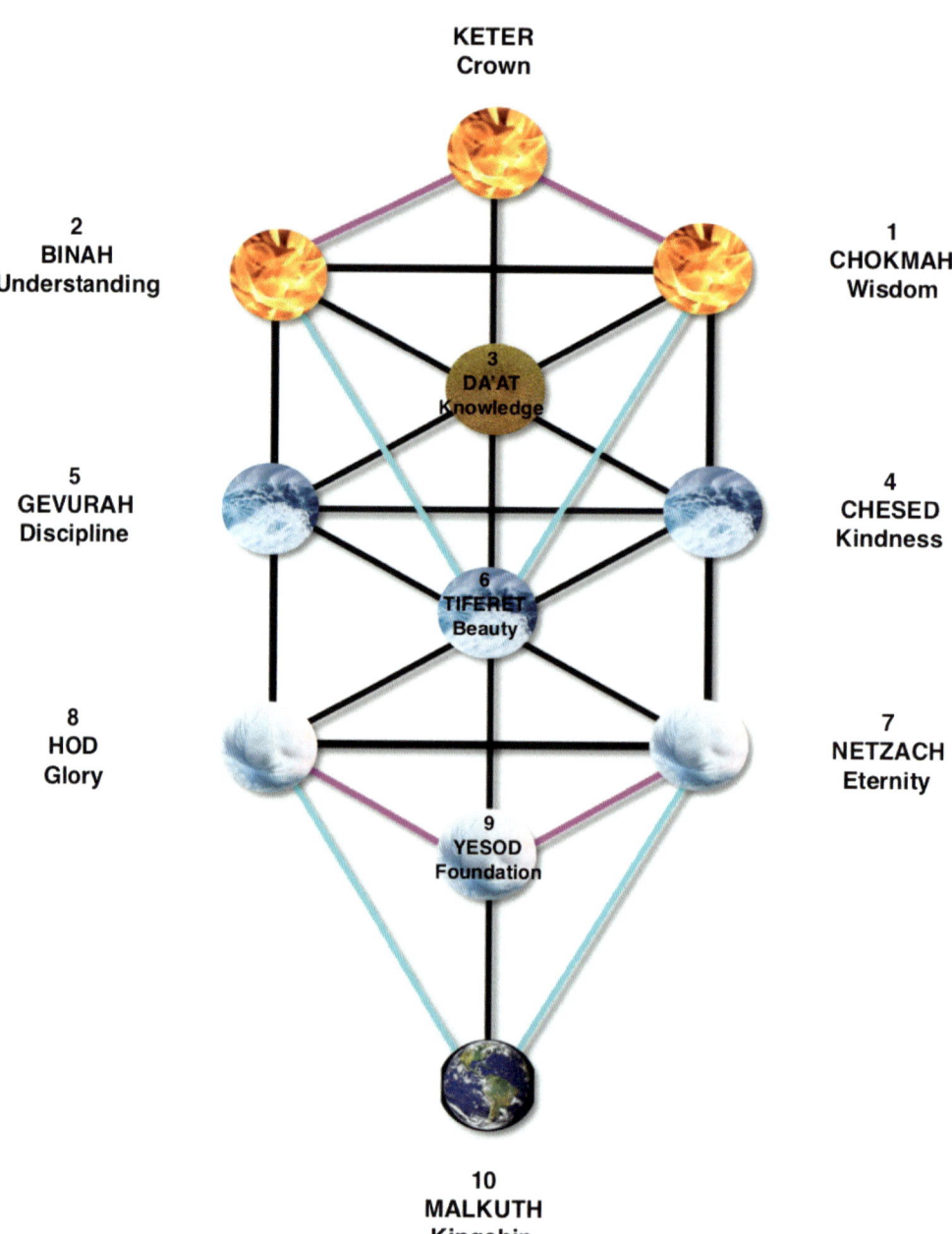

ILLUSTRATION 1 : "SEPHIROT TREE OF LIFE"

Artistic depiction by K C King - 03/2019

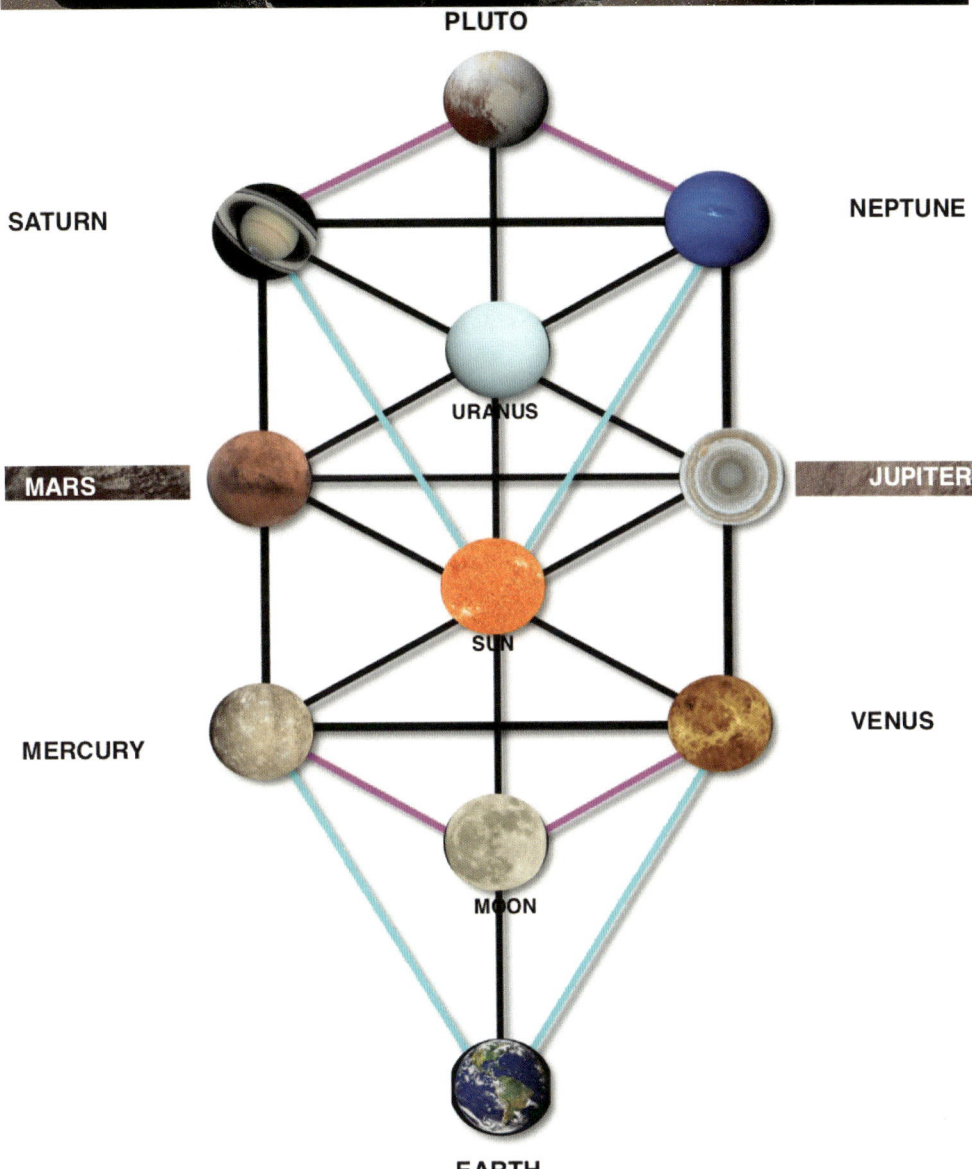

ILLUSTRATION 2 : "THE SOLAR SYSTEM"

Artistic depiction by K C King - 03/2019

We make the following affirmations daily, when we say "**The Lord's Prayer**" and reflect on it:

"Our Father who art in Heaven.
Hallowed be thy Name.
Thy Kingdom come, Thy will be done,
On Earth, as it is in Heaven.
Give us this day our daily bread. Forgive us our trespasses, as we forgive those who trespass against us.
Lead us not into temptation.
Deliver us from Evil.
For Thine is the Kingdom, the Power and the Glory.
Forever and Ever."
"Amen."

Therefore, each Sephirah corresponds not only to an outer divine function, but also an inner divine function and response.

For example, the Keter awakens will, delight and faith; whilst victory emanates inner confidence. I have found these inner responses or experiences, to be very similar to the fruits of the spirit as stated before.

In the the Catholic Vulgate Tradition listed in Chapter 5 of the Epistle to Galations there are 12 fruits: *charity, joy, peace, patience, benignity (kindness), goodness, longanimity (generosity), mildness (gentleness), faith, modesty, continency (self-control), and chastity.* These are tabulated overleaf. Parts of the Sephiroh also correspond to certain human body parts and organs. These in turn, are alignable with certain chakra energy systems.

TIER	SEPHIROT	OUTER EXPERIENCE	INNER EXPERIENCE	FRUIT OF THE SPIRIT	BODY PART
N/A	Keter	Super-conscious / Crown	Faith (Emunah), Delight (Taanug), Will (Ratzon)	Faith	N/A
1	Chokhmah	Wisdom	Selflessness (Bittul)	Charity	Right brain
2	Binah	Understanding	Joy (Simchah)	Joy	Left brain, Heart
3	Da'at	Knowledge	Union of ideas (Yichud)	Self-control, Peace	Central Brain
4	Chesed	Love +kindess	Divine Love (Ahavah)	Benignity, Patience	Right arm, hand
5	Gevurah	Might/Severity	Awe, or Fear of God (Yirah)	Via Chastity	Left arm, hand
6	Tiferet	Harmony	Balances compassion/ Mercy (Rachamin)	Mildness, Modesty, Generosity	Torso
7	Netzach	Victory/eternity	Confidence (Bitachon)	Via continency & self-control	Right leg, kidney
8	Hod	Thanksgiving	Sincerity (Temimut)	Benignity	Left leg, kidney
9	Yesod	Foundation	Truth (Emet)	Goodness.	Sexual organs
10	Malchut	Kingship	Basic Action (Shiflut)	Executed through "Gifts" of the spirit.	Mouth/ (Feet in some texts)

Table of The Sephirot and best corresponding "Fruits".

The "Keter", or "Kether", is the top-most Sephirot. **"The Keter" represents the Divine Superconscious which suprasses all.**

The Sephirot also represent Creation, as well as the act of union between husband and wife. This is a spiritual union, or marriage. It is an illustration of "The Elohim's" command to mankind to "be fruitful"; and to show love and honour by procreating in their "Image", and in their "Glory". It is representative of unity with the **Divine "Shechinah",** by divine union between male and female aspects. This is also representative of **"The Divine"** that shines through us, coming forth into the **Material World (Malkuth)**.

"The world and the souls in it, can be looked at as a 'Grail' that receives the Light. **However**, they can also give forth light and life of their own". Therefore,"**what is the Holy Grail *really* ?**"

There are **many** more possibilities of how the Sephirot could be interpreted and illustrated, of which this chapter is just **one**.

In essence, from the illustrations discussed in this chapter, one comes to the understanding that the "Tree of Life" is within one's self. "The Tree of Life **is** *you*, and is also ***within*** *you*." The emanations are reflected within you, and without. The attributes can all be found within yourself, and expressed through your actions and through your fruits. The Sephirots are mirrored in the elements, throughout the heavens, and throughout time. The Kabbalah system is ***highly*** complex, and there are many other Trees within its Greater Wisdom. In addition, like most things, there also exist shadow opposites. For example, "Good versus Evil"; or the "Tree of Life" versus the "Tree of Death", and so on.

Therefore, for the majority, and like within certain parts of this book, it is not the *minor* details that matter, but rather the main concept and the take home message that can be applied positively to everyday life.

Here the Parable of the Mustard Seeds, could also be applied. The tree with budding knowledge and wisdom being represented by **working towards the highest Sephirot (Malchut), and formulating good and wholesome things into action on this physical plane; having received the right nourishment.**

The archetypal world reminds us all that all things are possible through faith and will, and living in remembrance and the true image of "The Elohim", "Most High". Understanding this basic concept is the key to success throughout all planes, and aspects in life.

> *"YOU are the Tree of Life & the key to unlocking its Knowledge resides within you."*
>
> *- K C King 03/2019*

"Know that thou art the Greater Light,
perfect in thine own sphere..."
- *Emerald Tablets of Thot the Atlantean, Tablet 11*

CHAPTER 3
REPETITION & GROWTH

What is the meaning of recurring numbers , and why do some of us keep noticing them?

The truth is, for some, they will be just recurring numbers, **and just that.** But for others, they will be a code to something much more.

Your imagination is the strongest thing you have. With some creativity you can begin to unlock the meaning those recurring sequences may have in store for you.

A young girl kept seeing the same numbers on the way home. She kept asking herself, "Why do I keep seeing these same numbers on the buses, on the buildings, and on my time piece?"

She wrote them down, and began to ask questions. These then led to more questions. From here the next phase of her journey began.

THE KABALLAH

NUMBERS 1-10 : THE 10 AFFIRMATIONS OF THE ELOHIM

In Genesis, there are 10 affirmations that "The Elohim" made, in creating the World. These affirmations can be linked back to the Kabbalah, the Sephirot, and thus the Tree of Life. Below is a table that has been constructed depicting this information.

GENESIS REFERENCE (KJV)	BIBLE VERSE	SEPHIROT	TIER
Gen 1:3	"Let there be Light."	Kether	TOP
Gen 1:6	"Let there be a firmament in the midst of the Waters, and let it divide the Waters from the Waters."	Chokhmah	1
Gen 1:9	"Let the Waters under the heaven be gathered together unto one place, and let the dry land appear."	Binah	2
Gen 1:11	"Let the Earth bring forth grass, the herb yielding seed, and the fruit tree yielding fruit after his kind, whose seed is in itself, upon the earth."	Chesed	4
Gen 1:14-15	"Let there be lights in the firmament of the heaven to divide the day from the night; and let them be for signs, and for seasons, and for days, and years: And let them be for lights in the firmament of the heaven to give light upon the earth"	Gevurah	5
Gen 1:20	"Let the waters bring forth abundantly the moving creature that hath life, and fowl that may fly above the earth in the open firmament of heaven"	Tiferet	6
Gen 1:22	"Be fruitful, and multiply, and fill the waters in the seas, and let fowl multiply in the earth."	Netzach	7
Gen 1:26	"Let **us** make people in **our** image, after **our** likeness: and let them have stewardship over the fish of the sea, and over the fowl of the air, and over the cattle, and over all the earth, and over every creeping thing that creepeth upon the earth."	Hod	8
Gen 1:28	"Be fruitful, and multiply, and replenish the earth, and keep it: and have stewardship over the fish of the sea, and over the fowl of the air, and over every living thing that moveth upon the earth".	Yesod	9
Gen 1:29-30	"Behold, I have given you every herb bearing seed, which is upon the face of all the earth, and every tree, in the which is the fruit of a tree yielding seed; to you it shall be for meat. And to every beast of the earth, and to every fowl of the air, and to every thing that creepeth upon the earth, wherein there is life, I have given every green herb for meat. And it was so."	Malchut	10

Table of the 10 Affirmations of "The Elohim"

The letter 22 is important within the Kabbalah system. There are also 22 letters in the Traditional Hebrew alphabet. The Hebrew alphabet is particularly special because its letters can be combined and found in the "Star of David", and also in the "Sephirot Tree".

Number sequences can be found in the Sephirot Tree:

3 : There are three letters that represent the horizontal lines.

These are: *Aleph, Mem, and Shin.*

7 : There are seven letters representing the vertical lines.

These are: *Bet, Gimel, Dalet, Kaf, Pe, Resh, and Tav.*

12 : There are twelve letters representing the diagonal lines.

These are: *He, Vav, Zayin, Chet, Tet, Yod, Lamed, Nun, Samekh, Ayin, Tsade, and Qof.*

All together, these make up the 22 channels of the Sephirot Tree.

*This is illustrated in the spread between p 30 - 31.

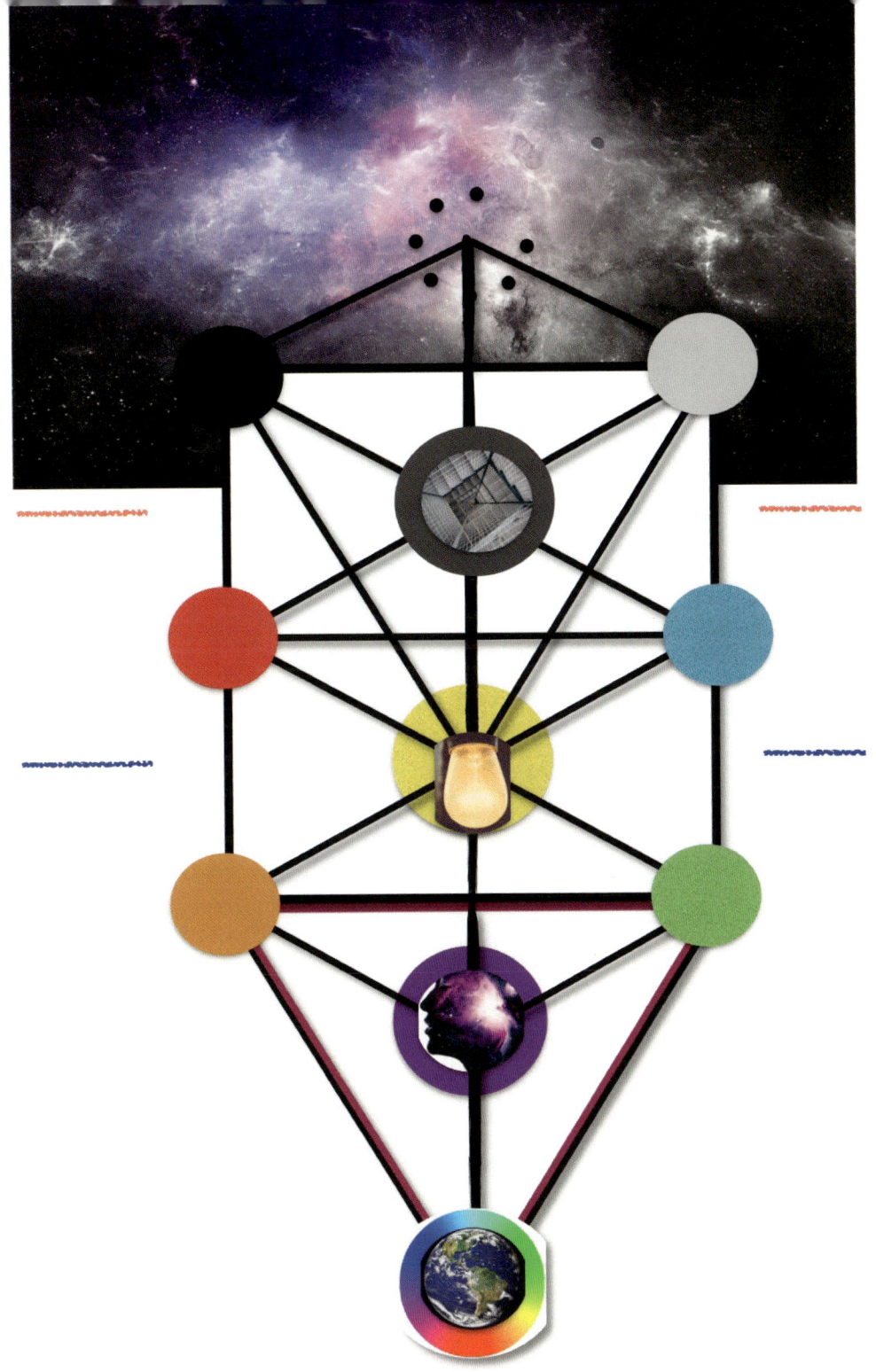

ILLUSTRATION 3 : "HEAVEN'S MIRRORS"

"...For thine is the Kingdom, the Power, and the Glory". "Amen".
Abstract Artistic depiction by K C King - 03/2019

THE HEBREW ALPHABET

Hebrew Letter	ח	ז	ו	ה	ד	ג	ב	א
Pronounciation	Chet	Zayin	Vav	He/ Hei	Dalet	Gimel	Bet/Vet	Aleph
Gematria	8	7	6	5	4	3	2	1
Phonetic	ch, x	z	v, w	h	d	g	b	Silent/ Glottal plosive

Hebrew Letter	ע	ס	נ	מ	ל	כ	י	ט
Pronounciation	Ayin	Samekh	Nun	Mem	Lamed	Kaf/ Kaph	Yud/Yod	Tet
Gematria	70	60	50	40	30	20	10	9
Phonetic	Silent/ Glottal plosive	s	n	m	l	k	j, y	t

Hebrew Letter	ת	ש	ר	ק	צ	פ
Pronounciation	Tav/ Taw	Shin	Resh	Kof/ Qof	Tzadi/ Tsade	Pe/ Fe
Gematria	400	300	200	100	90	80
Phonetic	t	f, s	r	k, q	ts	f, p

The hebrew lettering system is read from right to left. As shown above, there are two silent letters in the hebrew alphabet. When constructed into words, these two silent letters are normally associated with vowels.

There are different styles of hebrew writing, which vary depending on Sect. The Aramaic style *(Ketav STAM)*, written with a Quill, is preserved for sacred writing of the *Sifrei Torah, Tefillin, Mezuzot, and the Five Megillot.*

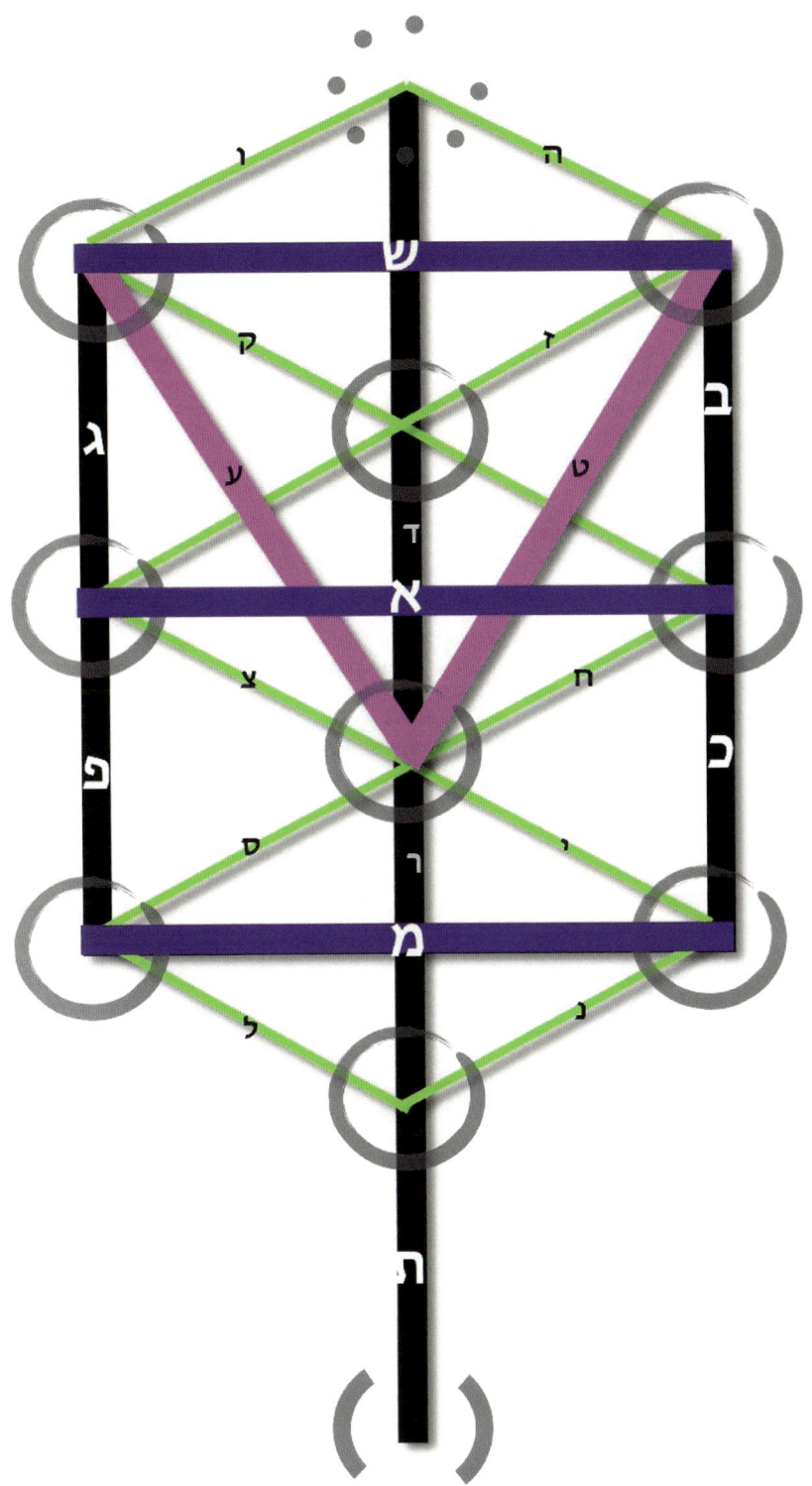

THE SEPHIROT TREE : HEBREW ILLUSTRATION

Second Title: "The Helix", by K C King 09/04/2019

ILLUSTRATIVE MEANINGS OF THE NUMBERS 1-13

"Three is the mystery, come from the great one,
Hear, and light on thee will dawn."
- Emerald Tablets of Thot the Atlantean, Tablet 11

Here are some illustrative examples of the significance of these recurring numbers. Both mundane and spiritual examples are given. Use them as a tool to expand your mind, and think of some of your own.

Some corresponding angelic frequency interpretations are written *in italic*. The strength of the **attribute** is doubled, if the number is doubled, and so on.

NUMBER	ATTRIBUTES	TRAITS	ILLUSTRATIVE EXAMPLES
1	Singularity Phallux *Focussing*	Masculine God-Head Leadership & Kingship	* "The ALL", "Adonai", "The Absolute", "The Source". One Pope. One President. One Mouth Major singular organs: Heart, Brain, and Liver
2	Dualities Co-operation *Relationships*	Feminine Creative Power Queenship Maternal	Pairs of organs: 2 ovaries, 2 lungs, 2 eyes, 2 ears Some endocrine glands are paired : 2 adrenal glands The Human DNA strand is a double helix 2 Vernal Equinoxes 2 is the smallest prime number
3	Complete *Team work*	Creative Growth The Soul	"The Holy Trinity" "Tripple Moon Goddess" 3 sides of a Triangle Thot - **The Thrice Great "Trismegistus"** 3: A division of 336, the number of times "Faith" appears in the Bible **(KJV)** 3rd Heaven of Paradise **(1 Corinthians 12: 2- 4)**
4	Perfection Directional Divinity Sacredness *Divine Guidance*	Dimensional The Body Reference Revelation	4th Dimension - Illusion of Time 4 sides and dimensions of a square box 4 Canopic Jars used in Ancient Egypt during the mummification process 4 Cardinal Directions 4 Major Seasons 4 Rivers of Eden **(Genesis 2: 10-14)** 4 Heads of the Cherubim **(Ezekiel 1: 5-11)** 4 Horsemen of the Apocalypse **(Revelation 6: 1-8)**
5	Versatility *Change* Circumferential Magic	Strength Severity Fear	5 Major Elements of the Universe (Taoist Cosmology) 5 Mystical Elements 5 Points of a Pentagram 5 Pillars of Islam (Islam) The "Perfect Fifth" - basis of Pythagorean tuning for musical instruments.

ברקיע השמים

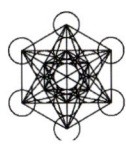

NUMBER	ATTRIBUTES	TRAITS	ILLUSTRATIVE EXAMPLES
6	Physicality *Spirituality*	Materialism Reflections	6 Days of Creation *(Genesis 1: 1-31)* 6th Element Carbon: has 6 protons, 6 electrons, 6 neutrons: 666 6 Sides to the Hexagram, Seal of Solomon or Star of David Hexagonal prismic cells of Honeycombs 6 Wings of the Seraphim *(Revelation 4:8)* The Number of Man & The Number of the Beast: 666. *(Revelation 13:18)*
7	Perfection Spirituality Christ - consciousness	Totality Universality Frequency Rest Security	7 days of the week 7th Sabbath Day/ Biblical Day of rest *(Genesis 2:2)* 7 Heaven's: *(7 "Shamayim" - Talmud), (Enoch 2 + 3), (Quran 71:15)*. 7 Hell's, "Naraka", or Underworlds (Jain Cosmology) 7 Interdimensional Planes or Levels (Hinduism) 7 Feast days of Saturnalia 7 Pillars of Wisdom *(Proverbs 9:1)* 7 "Gifts" of the Holy Spirit *(Isaiah 11:2-3)* 7: A division of 777: "Lamech", the father of Noah lived for 777 years.*(Gen 5: 28-31)*
8	Infinity *Perfection* Rebirth	Eternity Regeneration Possibilities *Abundance*	8 Sides to an Octagon 8: The atomic number of Oxygen 8: The number of legs of an Arachnid, e.g. the spider 8: The number of arms of an Octopus
9	Foundation *Pure intelligence* Circumferential	Celestial Perfection Triad	9 Deities of "The Great Ennead"(Ancient Egypt) 9 Mayan Underworlds 9 Months of Pregnancy "Thrice Three", Triple Goddesses (Celtic) 9: The highest number, before all other numbers are additions of each other
10	Divinity *Rebirth* Divine Kingdom	Law Order Dominion	10 Sephirot in the Tree of Life (Kabbalah) 10 Commandments *(Exodus 20: 1-17), (Deuteronomy 5: 4-12)* **10** - Gematria (numerical value) of "**YOD**" - the first letter for "**YHWY**" 10 Fingers and 10 Toes of the Human Body 10 Cubic Metres of the Cherubim *(1 Kings 6: 23-26)*
11	Power Equality *Spiritual Awakening	Masterful Neutral Insight	The smallest 2 digit prime number in the decimal system 11:11 - considered as a spiritual gateway or sign 11 sides of a Hendecagon 11 space-time dimensions in The String Theory Apollo 11: First Documented Moon Landing
12	Systems Patterns *Celestial*	Dimensional Cycles Heavenly	12 Days of Christmas (Yuletide) 12 Zodiac Constellations 12 Months in a Year *(Greco-Roman Calendar)* 12 Sons of Jacob *(Genesis 29 - 48)* 12 Tribes of Israel *(Genesis 49)* 12 Disciples of Christ *(Matthew 10: 2)* 12 Fruits of the Spirit *(Galatians 5:22-23, Vulgate)* 12 Foundation stones of the Holy City *(Exodus 28)* 12 Gates of Heaven *(Revelations 21:21)* 12 Stones on a Pharaohs Breast Plate *(Exodus 28; 15-21)*
13	*Sacredness*	Geometric Gateway	13 Circles in Metatron's Cube Individual numbers add up to 4 = Perfection 13th "Embolismic" Month of the Lunisolar Calendar 13 is a Fibonacci Number of Pascal's Triangle

CHAPTER FOUR

CHAPTER 4
BRANCHES OF ENERGY

THE CHAKRA SYSTEMS

The Chakra Systems corresponds to the systems of flow of **"Prana"** (similar to "Ch'i" or "Qi") energy in the body. These energy centres correspond to various organs in the body, and can be related to various physical and spiritual attributes.

Certain gemstones with similar metaphysical properties are often used in meditation to help with the flow of energies within their corresponding centres.

These are the **7 main chakra** systems used in Modern Western and Eastern conventional practices. The **"Kundalini" (Sanskrit)** or **"coiled-one"**, describes the **"divine life-force energy"** of this system, believed to sit in the basal chakra.

However, there are also systems within each system. For example, there are the 22 chakra points of Reflexology. These are also energy points, targeted in alternative medicine, massage and healing.

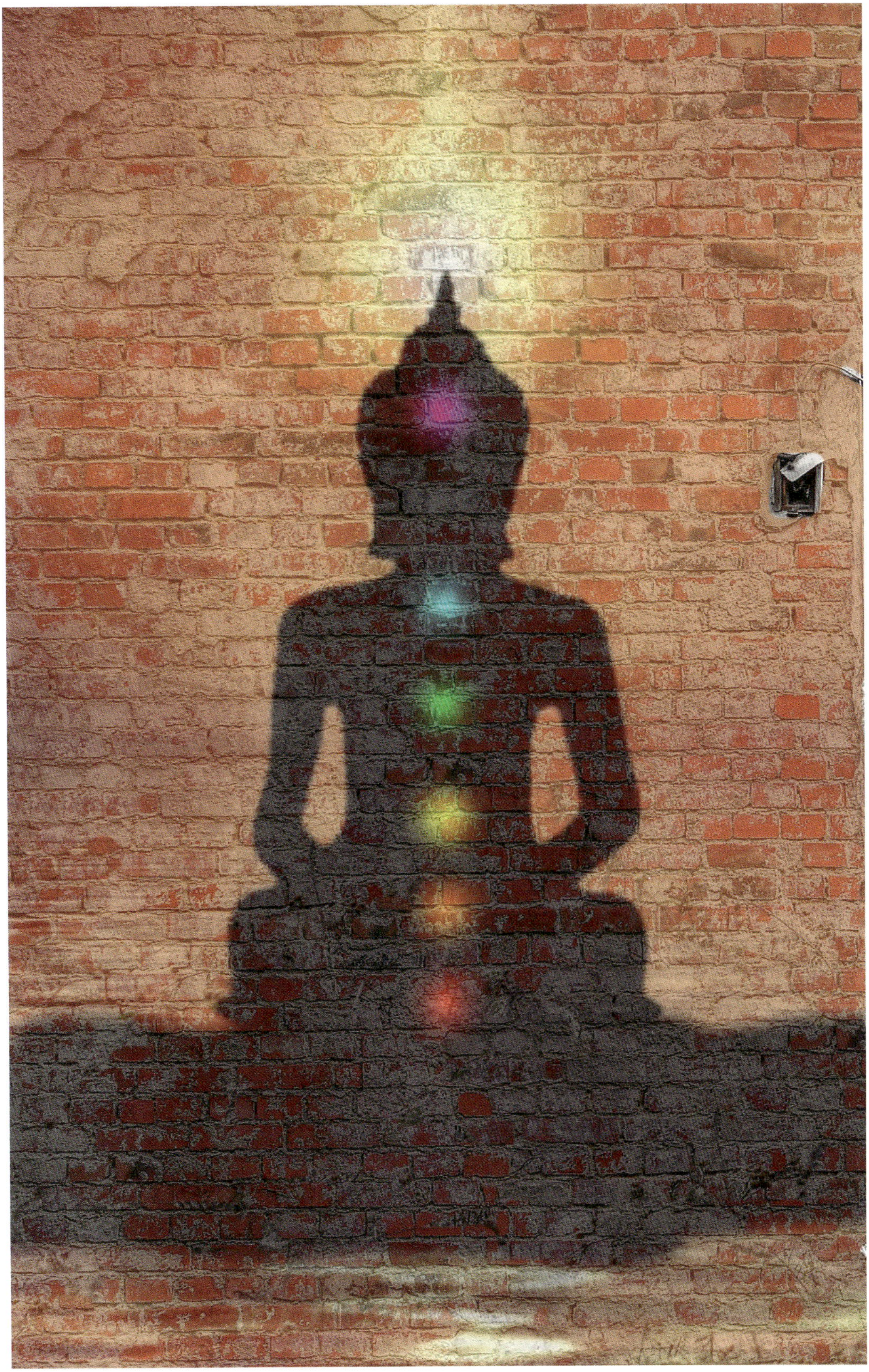

BRANCHES OF ENERGY

There a total of 52 individual elements of the Chakra system. Ultra Advanced spiritual systems go up to 36 Chakra levels, with **7 dimensional subdivisions**.

These reflect the concept of **"The Seven Heaven's"** or inter-dimsensional planes, and **"Oneness"** in attribute with the **"ALL"** or the **"Infinite Extreme"**.

Using the elements, it is also possible to plot and figure out the corresponding ruling planetary systems and zodiac signs for each chakra level. However, this exceeds the objectives of this book.

Everything can be linked back to corresponding fruits on a Celestial Tree.

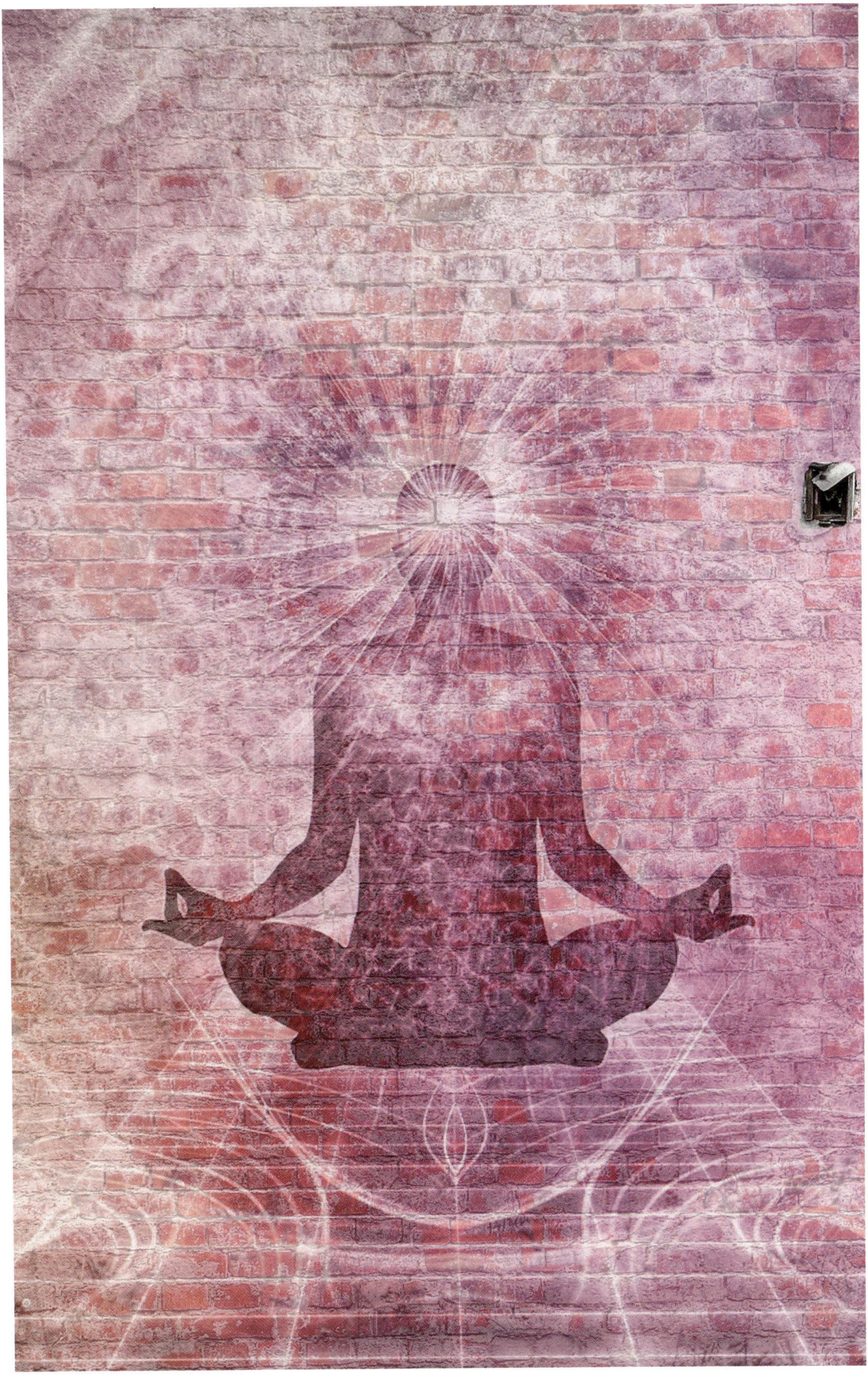

CHAKRA (Sanskrit)	SYMBOL	ORGANS	ATTRIBUTE	POLARITY	MANTRA	STONE (Examples)	ELEMENT
Crown Chakra (Sahasrara)		Pineal Gland	Spirituality	Spiritual Body Feminine /-ve	ANG	Amethyst	Spirit
Brow / Third Eye Chakra (Ajna)		Pituitary, Hypothalamus	Intuition	Spiritual Body Feminine /-ve	OHM	Lapiz lazuli, Amethyst	Light
Throat Chakra (Vishuddha)		Thymus, Thyroid	Communication	Mental Body Masculine /+ve	HAM	Lapiz Lazuli, Blue agate	Sound
Heart Chakra (Anahata)		Heart	Love	Emotional Body Masculine /+ve	YAM	Tourmaline, Rhodonite	Air
Navel/ Solar Plexus Chakra (Manipura)		Adrenals, Pancreas, Kidneys	Power	Emotional Body Masculine /+ve	RAM	Carnelian, Tiger Eye, Sapphire	Fire
Sacral Chakra (Swadhisthana)		Testes, Ovaries	Sexuality	Physical Body Feminine /-ve	VAM	Carnelian, Citrine	Water
Root Chakra (Muladhara)		Reproductive oragns	Survival	Physical Body Feminine /-ve	LAM	Red Jasper, Garnet	Earth

Table: Breakdown of Chakra Levels

There are many different Chakra Systems as mentioned before, and various advanced systems. There are also many different mantras, which are used in mediation. The purpose of the mantra, is to allow alignment of that particular chakra by means of the **"vibration"**, or the **"frequency" of the mantra** vocalised.

"Om" or **"Aum"** is the Sanskrit word for God. In Hinduism, it refers to the God "Brahman". Universally, it refers to the "Supreme Being", the **"ALL"** of Creation. Thus, it is also believed to be one of the most sacred syllables, as a premordial sound of "God".

There are also Visual Mandalas which help with meditation. These are looked at during a state of meditation, to help augment concentration and relaxation. Mandalas are often used in Buddhism, but have variations in other cultures. By helping one to focus one's attention, they thereby help in initiating a trance state.

Some Mandalas also have a deep spiritual meaning. In this way, they can also help in establishing a sacred space during meditation. Each Mandala has a different meaning and purpose. The Mandala depicted above, is a Rainbow Mandala of the Lotus Flower. The Sephirot Tree can also be overlayed into its centre.

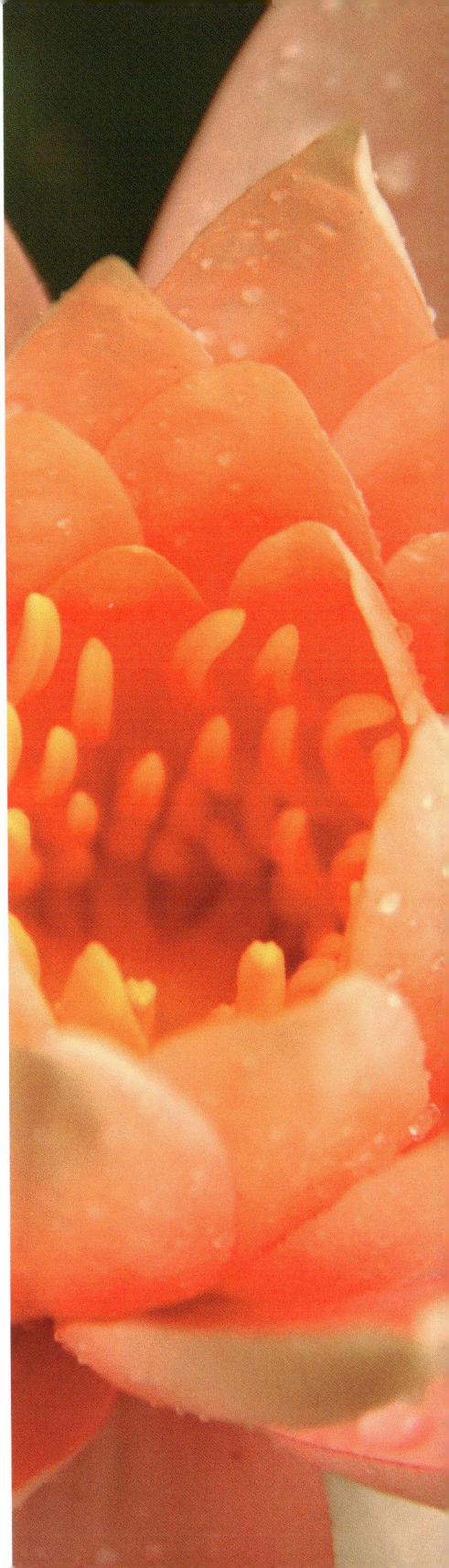

CHAPTER 5
FRUITS OF THE TREE

PRECIOUS STONES

In the Bible there are a large variety of precious stones with various physical and metaphysical properties. The use of these stones have spanned the ages, and have had many uses.

The Biblical High Priest's adorned their breastplates with a specific arrangement of such stones, for protection due to their properties, but also in memorial of the 12 Tribes of Israel *(Exodus 28: 15 - 21)*. The Ancient Egyptian Pharaohs also adorned their breastplates with various gemstones, not only for beauty and display of wealth, but for various metaphysical reasons also.

This section of this book, acts as an atlas demonstrating examples of these "biblical" stones and their properties.

CRYSTAL

Crystal is one of the major groups of precious stones.

There are many classes and types of crystal stones.

Crystal structures can also form in other substances such as :

 - Ice polycrystal structures when water freezes

 - Minerals such as sugar and salt.

- During the fossilisation of living organisms such as shells, producing organic crystals such as calcite.

Crystal was also one of the stones used in the breast plate of the High Priests; **and** before the Heavenly throne.

Biblical Verse: *"And in front of the throne there was something like a sea of glass, clear like crystal."*
- Revelation 4:6

DIAMOND

Modern Birth Month: April
Traditional Birth Month: April
Chakra Empowers: It can align all the chakras.

Physical properties: It is a pure form of carbon, formed under extremely high pressure deep under the earth's surface. The crystals form in a cubic structure - **cubic diamond**. Diamond forms in a range of colours including colourless to very dark or "black". **Diamond is the hardest structure, and the hardest crystal**; with a Mohs hardness rating of ten out of ten.

Metaphysical Properties: An historic gemstone. Believed to have strong talismanic properties due to its rare qualities. Unique ability to align all chakra centres. Deflects negative energy, and increases positivity.

Biblical Verse: *" The sin of Judah is engraved with a pen of iron, with the point of a diamond.." - Jeremiah 17:1*

SAPPHIRE

Modern Birth Month: September
Traditional Birth Month: April
Chakra Empowers: Throat
Physical properties: Many colours including blue.
Metaphysical Properties: Enhances communication & guidance, protection against psychic attacks.
Bible Verse: "*Her princes were purer than snow, whiter than milk; their bodies were more ruddy than coral, the beauty of their form was like sapphire.*"
– Lamentations 4:7

TOPAZ

Modern Birth Month: Nov/Dec.
Traditional Birth Month: Nov.
Chakra Empowers: All centres, depending on colour.
Physical properties: Multiple colours from yellow to purple. Raw state it is a golden brown/ yellow.
Metaphysical Properties: Empowers honesty, **trust**, loyalty. Protects from psychic attacks.
Biblical Verse:"*The topaz of Ethiopia cannot equal it, nor can it be valued in pure gold.*"-**Job 28:19**

EMERALD

Modern Birth Month: May.
*One of the few Traditional and Mystical Birth Stones, that has not been replaced.
Mystical Birth Month: January
Traditional Birth Month: May

Chakra Empowers: Heart Chakra
Physical properties: Pure Emerald crystal is often Apple Green in colour. It is also a variety of Beryl.

Metaphysical Properties:
Empowers patience, foresight and understanding. Balances the mood and senses.

Provides **strong** spiritual protection. Emerald was one of the stones used in the breast plate of the Pharaohs.

It was also used for protection in other settings in both Ancient Egypt and Greece.

Biblical Verse:
"The foundation stones of the city wall were adorned with every kind of precious stone, with the fourth as Emerald." —**Revelation 21:19**

RUBY

Modern Birth Month: July

Traditional Birth Month: December. Close in colour to Garnet as the stone for January.

Chakra Empowers: Heart

Physical Properties: Many colours. Commonly Red and Green.

Metaphysical Properties: Empowers courage. Enhances areas regarding love, passion, fertility, & mental health.

Biblical Verses:
"For wisdom is better than rubies, and all that you may desire cannot compare with her."
- Proverbs 8:11

" And there before me was a throne in Heaven... and the one who sat there, had the appearance of jasper and ruby."
- Revelation 4:2-3

AMETHYST

Modern Birth Month: February

Traditional Birth Month: February

Chakra Empowers: Crown Chakra

Physical properties: Light to Dark Purple or Violet Gemstone. It is a pure type of quartz crystal.

Metaphysical Properties: Fortifies spiritual connection, and enhances spiritual communication channels.

Combats mental health disorders such as depression, anxiety, mood disorders, and stress. Helps in cleansing and consecration of sacred spaces.

Biblical Verse: *"As for the foundation-stones of the city wall, the twelfth is amethyst."*
- Revelation 21:21

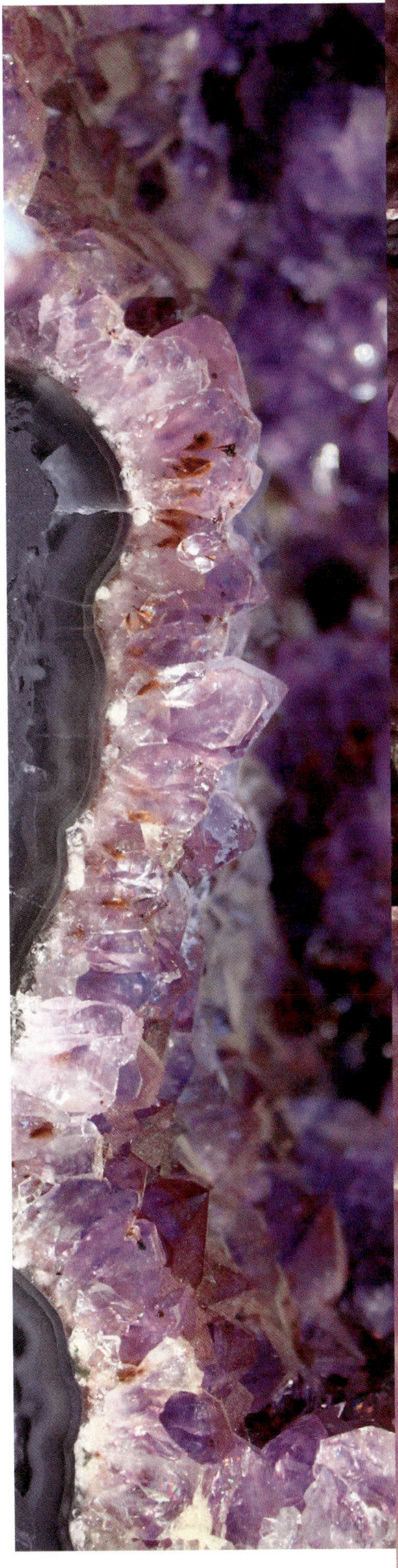

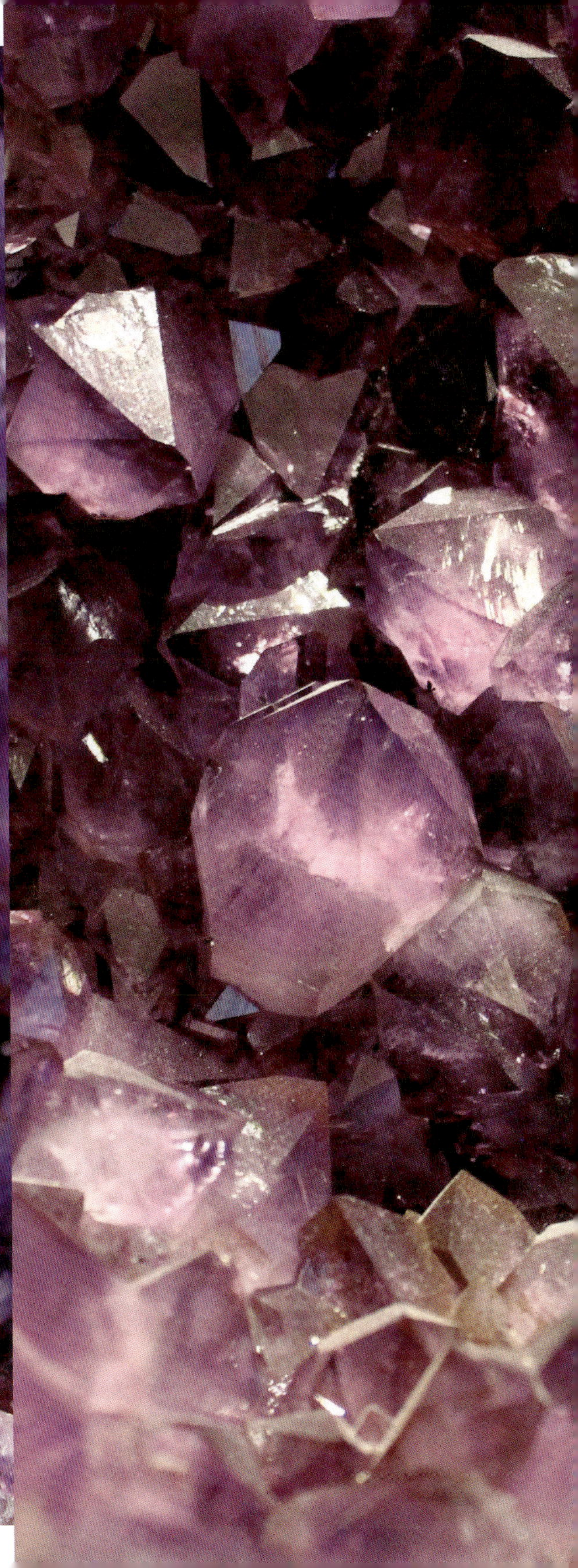

CHALCEDONY

Modern Birth Month: All the months except January, April, and November.

Zodiac: All the signs except Taurus, Cancer, Scorpio and Sagittarius.

Chakra Empowers: All levels of the Chakra depending on stone.

Physical properties :
Found worldwide. It describes a **group of stones** made of a microcrystalline or cryptocrystalline variety of quartz.

Chalcedony is found in almost every colour.

Metaphysical Properties
Wide array of Metaphysical properties, as it describes a group of stones.

There are many varieties of Chalcedony.

Examples of these include the following:

- Agate

- Aventurine

- Carnelian

- Chrysoprase

- Jasper

- Onyx

- Sardonyx

- Tiger's Eye

Biblical Verse:

"*As for the foundation-stones of the city wall, the third is chalcedony.*"

– ***Revelation 21:19***

AGATE

Modern Birth Month: Replaced by Emerald (May). Replaced by Moonstone & Pearl (June)

Traditional Birth Month: May & June

Chakra Empowers: Multiple depending on colour of Agate.

Physical properties: A variety of chalcedony, formed from layers of quartz which usually show various coloured bands. Varieties include: moss agate, and plume agate. Agate typically forms as rounded nodes or veins.

Metaphysical Properties: Dispels evil spirits and energies.

Biblical Verse: *"And have made of agate thy pinnacles, And thy gates of carbuncle stones, And all thy border of stones of delight."* **– Isaiah 54:12**

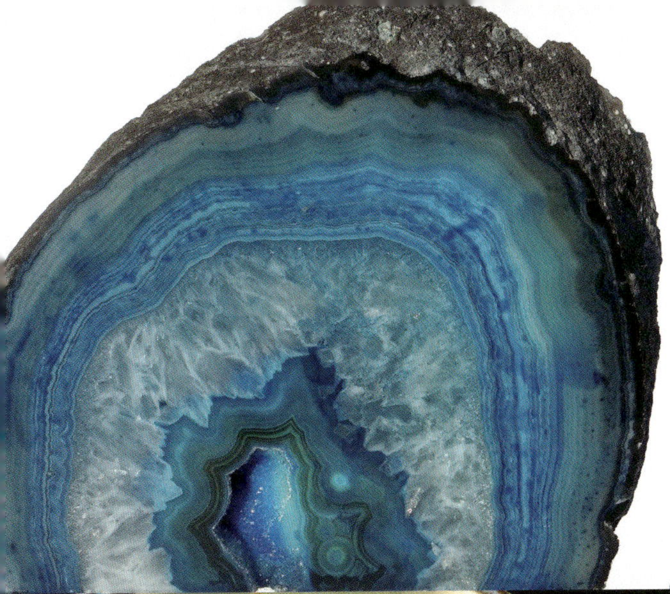
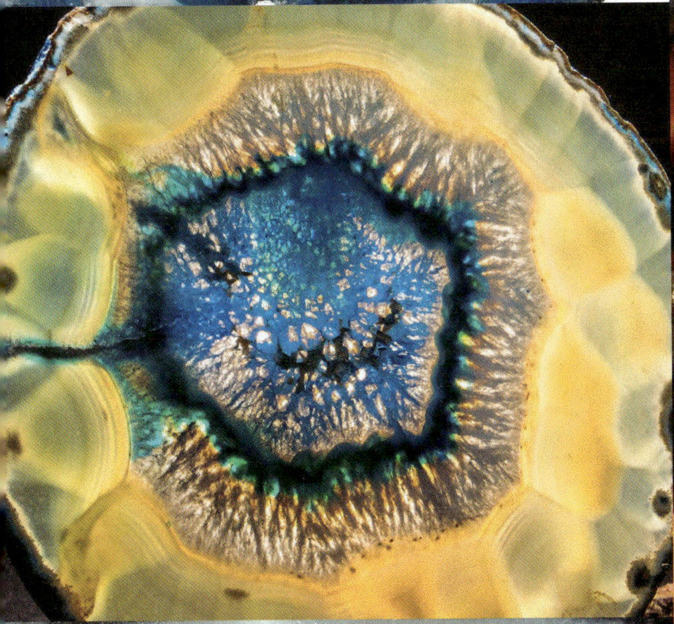
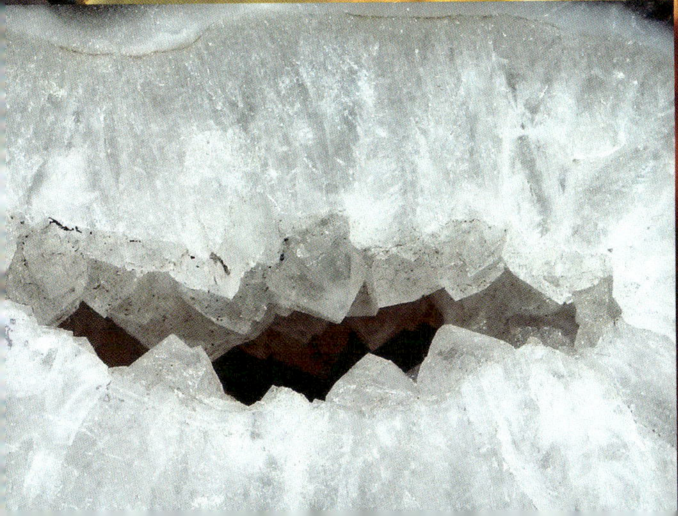
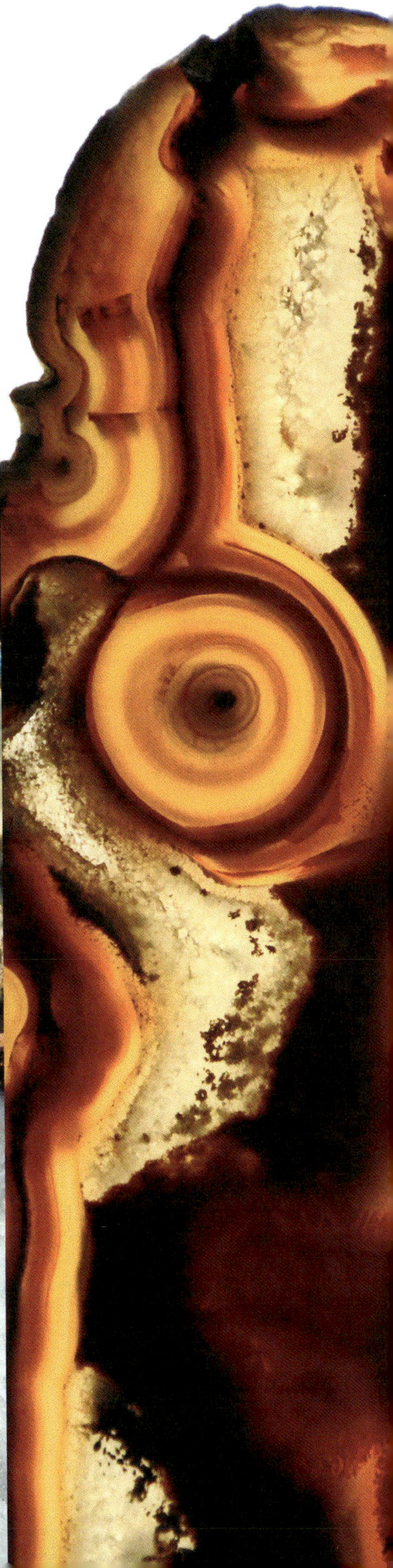

CARNELIAN

Modern Birth Month: July

Traditional Birth Month: Aug

Chakra: Sacral/Root

Physical properties: Shades of orange to blood red.

Metaphysical Properties: Empowers positive action, good decision making & life force-energy.

In Ancient Egypt, it was called the "Setting Sun".

Protected the dead during passage in the under world.

Also referred to as the stone of the Divine Feminine.

Biblical Verse:

"Place a setting of gemstones on it, four rows of stones: The first row should be a row of carnelian."
- Exodus 28:17

CHRYSOPRASE

Modern Birth Month: Replaced by Emerald for May

Traditional Birth Month: May

Chakra Empowers: Heart Chakra

Physical properties: Green chalcedony (cryptocrystalline quartz). Can be apple green. Called blood stone if it contains flecks of red.

Metaphysical Properties: Empowers fertility and trust. Balances emotions and energies.

Biblical Verse:

"As for the foundation-stones of the city wall, the tenth is chrysoprase."

- Revelation 21:21

JASPER

Modern Birth Month: Replaced by Aquamarine

Traditional Birth Month: March

Chakra Empowers: It can align all the chakras. Balances yin and yang.

Physical properties: "Speckled stone". An opaque, speckled type of chalcedony, or impure silica. It is found in a wide variety of colours; though blue jasper is rarer.

Metaphysical Properties: Jasper is protective. Jasper creates cleansing energies. It encourages enthusiasm and positive motivation.

Biblical Verse: *"A throne was set in Heaven... And he that sat was to look upon like a jasper and a sardine stone: and there was a rainbow round about the throne, in sight like unto an emerald."*

– Revelation 4:2-3

ONYX

Modern Birth Month: Replaced by Ruby

Traditional Birth Month: February

Chakra Empowers: Heart Chakra, Brow and Crown Chakras

Physical properties: A type of chalcedony, which is typically made up of a mixture of black and white bands. However, it can be found in a variety of colours.

Metaphysical Properties: Promotes regeneration. It empowers happiness, and spiritual intuition. It is also provides good spiritual protection.

Biblical Verse :

"And thou shalt take two onyx stones, and grave on them the names of the children of Israel."

– Exodus 28:9

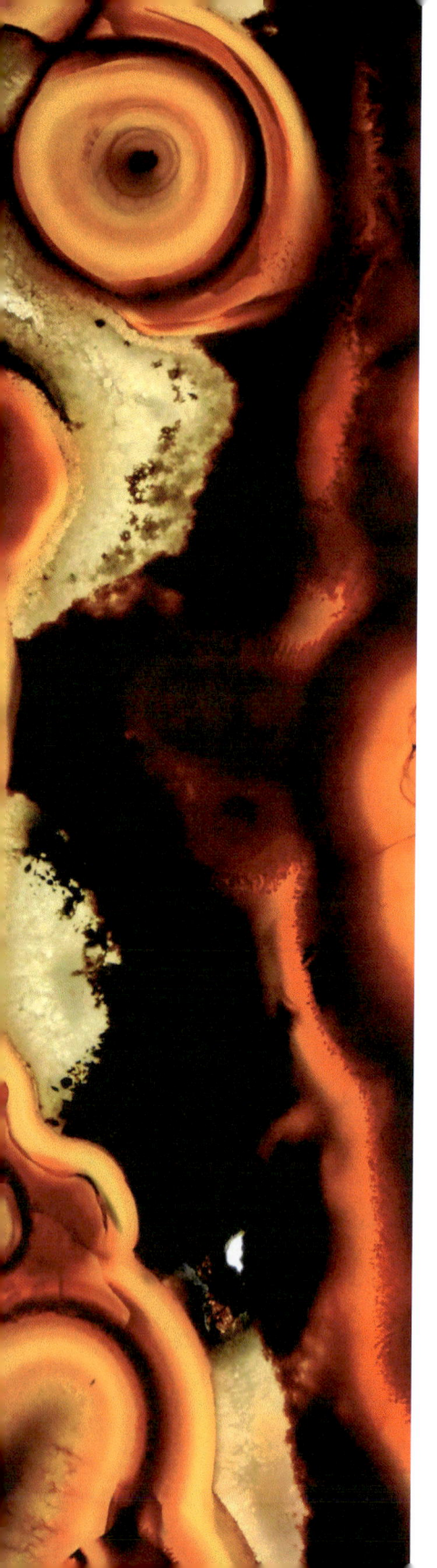

SARDONYX

Modern Birth Month: Replaced by Peridot.

Traditional Birth Month: August

Chakra Empowers: Root and Sacral Chakras

Physical properties: Sardonyx contains blends of onyx, chalcedony and carnelian. It is thought of as a variant of onyx, that has coloured bands which are shades of red ("sard"), rather than black. Sardonyx is a powerful stone due to its combination of properties.

Metaphysical Properties:
Highly protective stones from outside influences, for security and protection. Empowers fame, dignity and success.

Biblical Verse:
" And the foundations of the wall of the city were garnished with all manner of precious stones...the fifth [is] sardonyx".
- Revelation 21:19-20

OTHER STONES
CHRYSOLITE (PERIDOT)

Modern Birth Month: August

Traditional Birth Month: September

Chakra Empowers: Throat

Physical properties: Yellowish to green olive.

Metaphysical Properties: Increases luck and wisdom.

Biblical Verse:
"His hands gold rings, set with the chrysolite; His belly is bright ivory, overlaid with sapphires."
– Songs of Solomon 5:14

BERYL

Modern Birth Month: October

Traditional Birth Month: Nov

Chakra Empowers: Heart

Physical properties: Pure Beryl is colourless. Beryl is composed of the mineral beryllium aluminium cyclosilicate.

Beryl forms in a variety of colours depending on impurities.

Beryl is often found in emerald green (Chromium), golden yellow (Fe^{3+} ions), and aquamarine (Fe^{2+} ions).

Metaphysical Properties: Used in warding off evil spirits & jinn. Promotes cheerfulness and youthfulness.

Biblical Verse: "*Then they made the beryl stones, fixed in twisted frames of gold and cut like the cutting of a stamp, with the names of the children of Israel.*"
– *Exodus 39:6*

JACINTH (HYACINTH)
Not to be confused with the Hyacinth Flower.

Modern Birth Month: Replaced by Sapphire

Traditional Birth Month: September

Chakra Empowers: Crown Chakra

Physical properties: An orange-red transparent variety of zircon.

Metaphysical Properties: Was used as the first stone of the third row in the High Priest's breastplate, for potent spiritual protection. Also a foundational stone.

Biblical Verse: *"As for the foundation-stones of the city wall, the eleventh is jacinth."* - **Revelation 21:21**

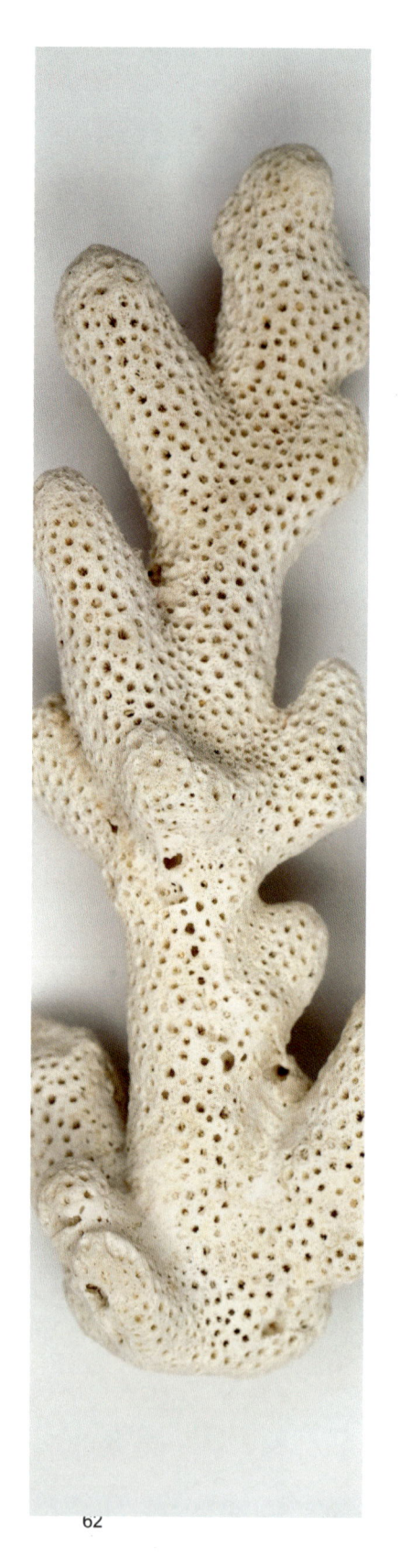

CORAL

Not a traditional birthstone.

Empowers Chakra: Heart and Root

Physical properties Extremely fragile and soft. Formed in the sea by the skeletal remains secreted by marine coral polyps. Thus made of primarily calcium carbonate.

Metaphysical Properties Enhances love life. It increases the strength to transform thinking positively. Coral also helps balance emotions.

Biblical Verse - *" Her consecrated ones were purer than snow, They were whiter than milk; They were more ruddy in body than corals."*

– Lamentations 4:7

PEARL

Modern Birth Month: February replaced by Amethyst. November replaced by Citrine.
Traditional Birth Month: February & November
Chakra Empowers: Brow
Physical Properties: Natural pearls are typically formed within living shelled mollusk. They are composed of calcium carbonate (in minute crystalline form), which has been deposited in concentric layers. Pearls can also be artificially manufactured.
Metaphysical Properties: Helps in maintaining spiritual clarity, insight and divination.

Biblical Verse: *"The gold of that land is pure; pearls and lapis lazuli are also there."* **–Gen 2:2**

Quranic Verse: *"God will admit those who believe and work righteous deeds, to Gardens beneath which rivers flow: they shall be adorned therein with bracelets of gold and pearls; and their garments there will be of silk."* **- 22:23**

LAPIS LAZULI

Modern Birth Month: Sept
Traditional Month: Dec.
Chakra Empowers: Throat Chakra, Third Eye Chakra
Physical properties:
Combination of various minerals including lazurite, calcite (white), sodalite (blue) and pyrite (a metallic yellow). It is considered more of a rock. Lapis Lazuli forms as a strong blue, sometimes with a hint of violet. Sourced from Afghanistan, Siberia, Chile, and some parts the United States.

Metaphysical Properties:
Enhances spiritual intuition, understanding and creativity. Promotes relaxation and thereby aids sleep.

Biblical Verse:
"Now above the expanse that was over their heads, there was something resembling a throne, like lapis lazuli in appearance; and on that which resembled a throne, high up, was a figure with the appearance of a man."
- Ezekiel 1:26

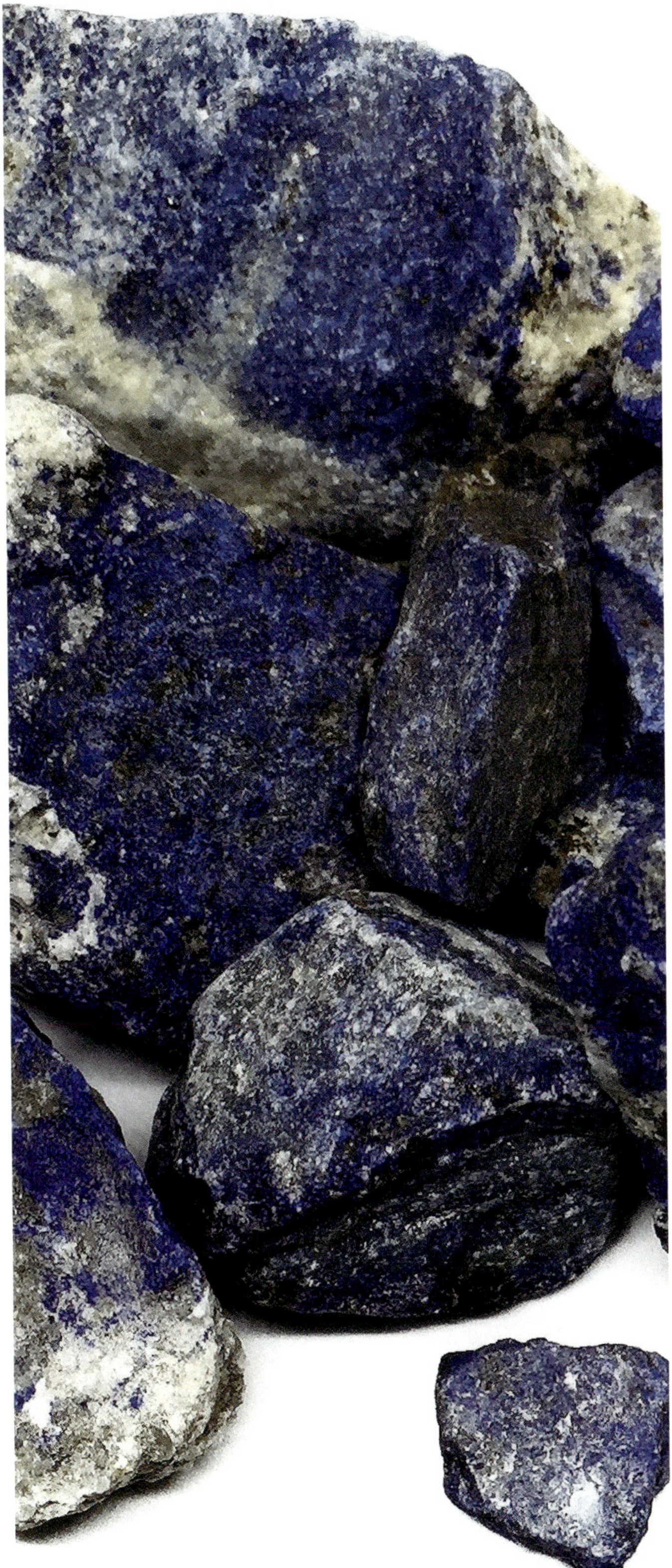
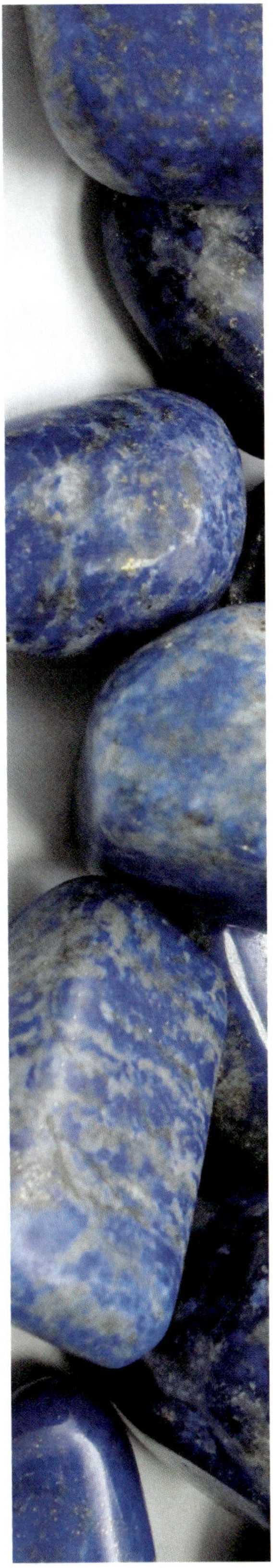

DREAMS

CHAPTER SIX
DREAMS

"Once upon a time, there was a young girl who fell in love, with everything she saw.

The absolute love, for the Most High's Creation, had her in awe.

Once upon a time, there was a girl who lived on cloud Nine.

The view from there, was Heavenly and Divine.

Once a upon a time, there was a young girl, who seemed stuck on this plane.

There she was taught, that Heaven and Earth could be the same. "

- K C King
(27/03/2019)

Dream BIG

Often the greatest ideas have come from dreams.

"Never let anyone kill your dream."

If someone tells you: "your dream is too small", then "dream bigger".

"If someone tells you, or has told you that your dream is too big, then dream <u>HUGE</u>".

They **first key** is to not let the opinions of others, change the dream that <u>*you*</u> want to have.

The **second key** is to have the **will** to pursue that dream.

The **third key** is to know and understand, that not **all** dreams come true, but that you can **always start dreaming again**.

*"Imagination is more important than knowledge.
Knowledge is limited.
Imagination encircles the world".*
- Albert Einstein, 1929

Whatever you focus on will be brought to you in various ways.

For example, when you sing and give praise, the vibrations and frequency of that song, are manifested by the thoughts and emotions that you subsequently feel. **Therefore, "enjoy your dreams".**

Because, in life, if you focus on negative things all the time, you will always experience negativity.

Focus on positive things in your life, or how to transmute negative experiences into positive outcomes. That way you can attract more positive things into your life. It is also therefore, important to remember to give thanks, for all of life's experiences, **always.** My next book **"Remembrance"** will go more into this.

I have learnt that when you start taking things for granted, the Universe has a way of making you appreciate them again ! Additionally, if pain did not exist, would you really know what happiness and joy was, and be able to appreciate them?

"...Learn to think..."

CHAPTER SEVEN: CELESTIAL MIRRORS

> *"Look thee above or look thee below,*
> *the same shall ye find.*
> *For all is but part of the Oneness*
> *that is at the Source of the Law.*
> *The consciousness below thee is*
> *part thine own as we are a part of thine"*
> *- The Emerald Tablets, Tablet 11*

In Judeo-Christian doctrine there were 12 disciples. In the Roman calendar there are 12 months of the year. The number 12 seems to recur in many systems.

In Western Astrology, there are also 12 zodiac astrological signs. These also correlate to certain star systems or "constellations". The names of the zodiac (or horoscope) signs are derived from the shapes of interconnecting lines within these star systems.

The "sky", or "celestial hemispheres", has been divided into a total of 88 constellation systems, 12 of these belong to the zodiac group of stars. This division was created by The International Astronomical Union. The zodiac division is based on the Annual "Ecliptic" or "Circular" movement of the Sun in relation to the Earth.

The 12 Zodiac Divisions are: *Aries, Taurus, Gemini, Cancer, Leo, Virgo, Libra, Scorpio, Sagittarius, Capricorn, Aquarius and Pisces.* **The Astrological Calendar begins with Aries in March.** This marks the point of the beginning of Spring, or the end of Winter. It is used as a reference point across many systems. It is also called the **"Spring Equinox"**, "Vernal" (Northern Hemisphere), or "Autumnal Equinox" (Southern Hemisphere). There is an overlap of the Spring Equinox, with Lent, Passover and Easter Celebrations.

The strength, or dominance of each sign also varies depending on its astrological alignment throughout the year. Each sign has its "opposite" or " astrological couple". These thus form a total of **six Zodiac Pairs**. <u>**These are as follows, in order:**</u> *(1) Aries & Libra, (2) Taurus & Scorpio, (3) Gemini & Sagittarius, (4) Cancer & Capricorn, (5) Leo & Aquarius, and (6) Virgo & Pisces.*

71

Due to the movements of these celestial bodies, each zodiac division, also has a corresponding planet, for that constellation of stars. This information is reflected in the following table.

TABLE: ZODIAC SIGNS & THEIR CORRESPONDING BODIES

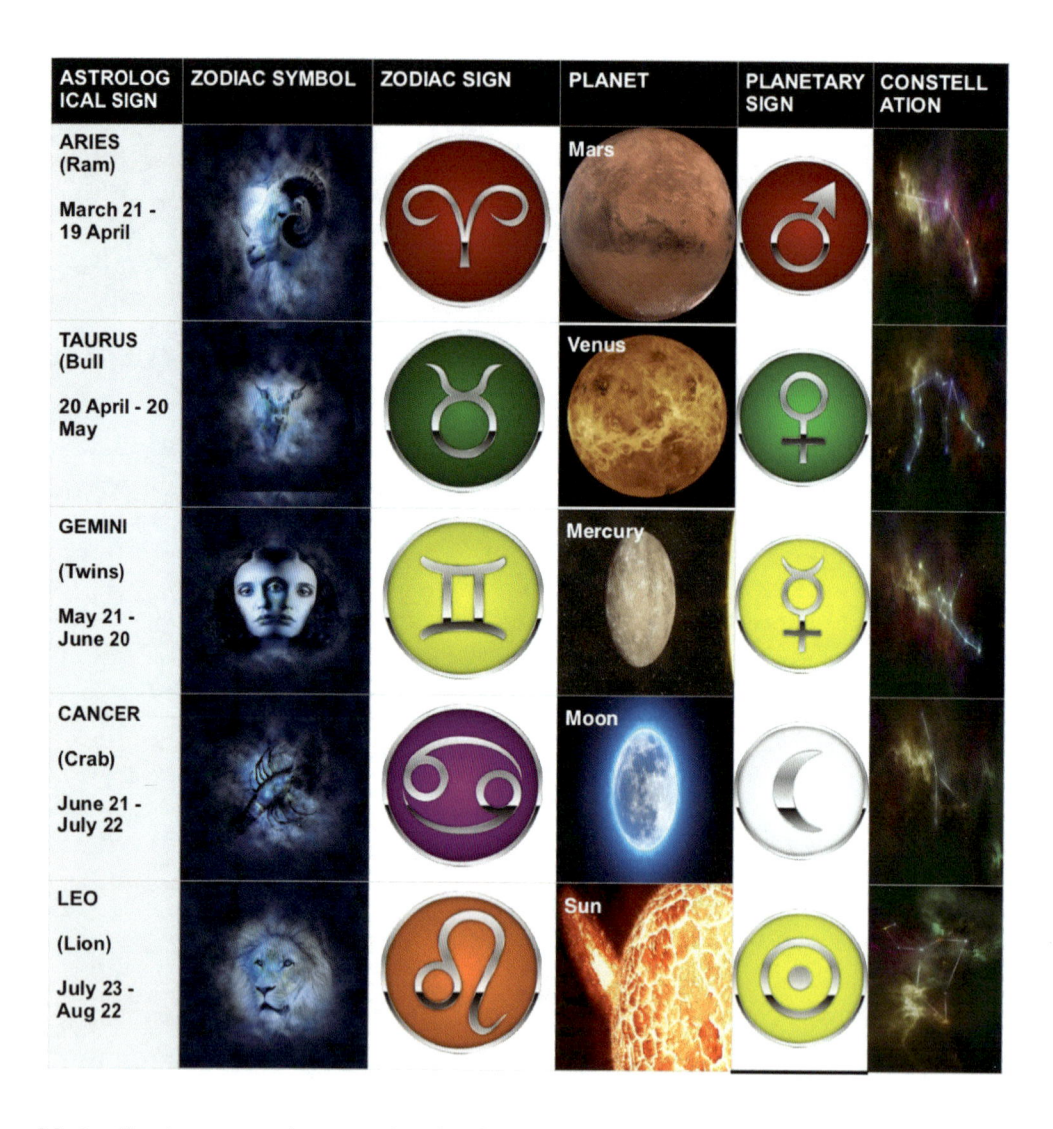

ASTROLOGICAL SIGN	ZODIAC SYMBOL	ZODIAC SIGN	PLANET	PLANETARY SIGN	CONSTELLATION
ARIES (Ram) March 21 - 19 April			Mars		
TAURUS (Bull) 20 April - 20 May			Venus		
GEMINI (Twins) May 21 - June 20			Mercury		
CANCER (Crab) June 21 - July 22			Moon		
LEO (Lion) July 23 - Aug 22			Sun		

Note that, as each astrological group has a corresponding pictographic zodiac sign and symbol; each corresponding planet has also been given a certain reference sign, for ease in astrological use. These are used in astrological charting.

ASTROLOGICAL SIGN	ZODIAC SYMBOL	ZODIAC SIGN	PLANET	PLANETARY SIGN	CONSTELLATION
VIRGO (Maiden) Aug 23- Sep 22			Mercury		
LIBRA (Scales) Sep 23 - Oct 22			Venus		
SCORPIO (Scorpion) Oct 23 - Nov 21			Pluto (previously Mars)		
SAGITTARIUS (Centaur) Nov 22 - Dec 21			Jupiter		
CAPRICORN (Goat) Dec 22 - Jan 19			Saturn		
AQUARIUS (Water bearer) Jan 20 - Feb 18			Uranus (classically Saturn)		
PISCES (Fish) Feb 19 - Mar 20			Neptune (classically Jupiter)		

The **"Angelic Number"** corresponds to one's **"House Ruling"**, depending on what text you are reading, and under what context. One's angelic number, corresponds to a special numeric frequency. This is similar to how one's name, can amount to a special numeric meaning in sacred numerology. A perfect example of this that we looked at was " יהוה ".

Each Hebrew letter has a corresponding numeric equivalent. The frequency of these numbers also give special power to the Four Letter Divine Name of God, or other names of God. Therefore, in simplest of terms, this section demonstrates, how a name can transmit a certain *frequency*.

On constructing the table, one can appreciate that the ruling elements for a particular zodiac sign also seem to occur in a pattern. This is most appreciated from the second house downwards. Of note, the fire element only recurs twice, and air occurs the most, having an occurrence of four. On a mundane level, air is a fuel source for fire.

There are numerous angel systems assigned to each astrological sign, of which the planetary system of Angels is just one. Regarding the objectives of this book, I have just briefly touched on this in the forthcoming table.

The Pentagram of Five Elements below, depicts the five physical elements. The Pentagram has many uses, across many mystical and spiritual circles.

Though its looks simple, similar to the Hexagram, it is an extremely complex symbol, and should not be used without great understanding. This is important, as like the zodiac signs, even the pentagram has its opposite.

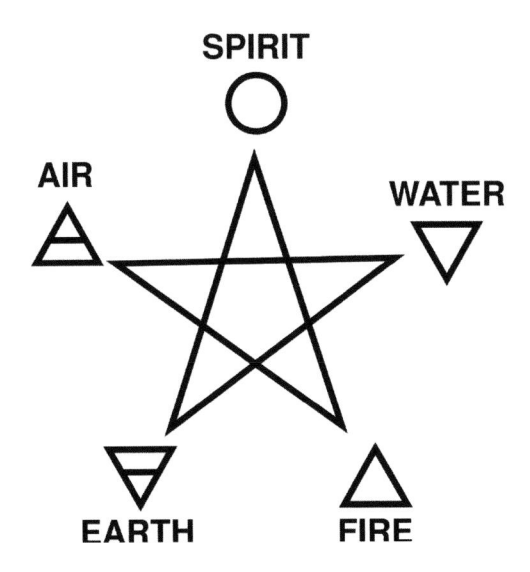

```
            SPIRIT
              O
   AIR        △
    △                WATER
                      ▽

         ▽        △
       EARTH    FIRE
```

The fifth element of spirit, can represent, for the purposes of this book, the spirit of the individuals across across each zodiac alignment; as this is the only element not found written in conventional zodiac charts.

TABLE: ASTROLOGICAL SIGN WITH CORRESPONDING RULINGS, ELEMENTS AND TRAITS

ASTROLOGICAL SIGN	PLANETARY ANGEL	ELEMENT	TRAITS (*EXAMPLES)	HOUSE RULING
AIRES (03/21 - 04/19)	Camael	Air	Assertive, Active	1
TAURUS (04/20 - 05/20)	Hanael	Earth	Devoted, Willful	2
GEMINI (05/21 - 06/20)	Raphael	Air	Communication. Logic based on Dualities	3
CANCER (06/21 - 07/21)	Gabriel	Water	Nurturing, Protective	4
LEO (07/23 - 08/22)	Michael	Fire	Creative, Leaders	5
VIRGO (08/23 - 09/22)	Raphael	Earth	Analytical, Orderly	6
LIBRA (09/23 - 10/22)	Hanael	Air	Balance between polarities, Intuitive	7
SCORPIO (10/23 - 11/21)	Asrael	Water	Transformative, Deep perception	8
SAGITARRIUS (11/22 - 12/21)	Zadkiel	Fire	Optimistic, Humorous	9
CAPRICORN (12/22 - 01/19)	Cassiel	Earth	Ambitious, Driven	10
AQUARIUS (01/20 - 02/18)	Auriel	Air	Sociable, Networking	11
PISCES (02/19 - 03/20)	Zadkiel	Water	Intuitive, Imaginative	12

*My next book "Remembrance" will go more into the attributes of each Angel.

WHAT IS A CELESTIAL PLANISPHERE?

The origins of the earliest constellations, are found in many ancient stories, and go back to pre-documented history.

Different cultures over the ages, have adopted their own constellations, with some variation over history. These would be documented in what is called a "Celestial Planisphere".

There are 88 modern star constellations. These were verified by the the International Astronomical Union (IAU) in 1928. The IAU includes >12,000 professional astronomers from over 90 countries worldwide.

The IAU is a member of the International Council for Science (ICS). The ICS, is in turn, an international organisation, that is devoted to international agreements in the advancement of science.

What is the purpose of the Constellation System?

The aim of the constellation system is to enable division of the celestial body into identifiable reference fields.

36 out of the 88 recognised constellations, lie predominantly in the northern hemisphere.

The other 52, are charted in the southern hemisphere.

Even throughout biblical times, the stars have been used as reference for many things, including travel.

The story of the **"Three Wise Men"**, was also a symbolic story representing this (see overleaf).

This book has focussed mostly on the 12 zodiac constellations for relevance.

A standard celestial atlas would include 30 plates, comprising of 26 constellation maps.

THE STAR OF DAVID AND THE THREE WISE MEN

It could be hypothesised, that the "Three Wise Men" of the Biblical Era **(Gospel of Matthew)** were referring to a specific configuration of stars, that only they, or people like them would have been able to recognise, especially during that time period.

The three wise men, who were in fact "Magi", used the "**Star of Bethlehem",** as a guiding star on their long journey from Jerusalem to Bethlehem. There, they were known to have offered gifts of Frankinsence, Myrrh and Silver to the "New Born King", of the Family of David.

Was the Star of Bethlehem a single star, or a very specific juxtaposition of several stars and planets, such as the Moon, Sun, and specific planets such Venus, Mercury and Jupiter; that would have occurred during that time period?

There are many speculations. Some artistic depictions, illustrate the star in various forms, such as a comet, or a single extra bright star over the Nativity scene. **However, the main learning point is, that the story demonstrates an historic use of Stars and their constellations, as celestial guiding systems**.

CELESTIAL ATLAS: INTRODUCTION

The "Index" will mainly focus on the 12 zodiac constellations for relevance.

The following section called **"ATLAS"** is a pictographic illustration to represent what the celestial charting for each of the 12 zodiac signs we have discussed would look like. They, and maps such as these, are beautiful in their own right, in my opinion, as independant works of art.

Have some fun later, star gazing, to see whether you can spot any of the "star territories".

Remember, a "full" celestial atlas would include at least 30 plates.

HISTORY OF THE CELESTIAL ATLAS

The first Western Celestial Atlas was published in 1822 in the Victorian Era. A slightly later and more colourful publication, **"Urania's Mirror"**, influenced by the first, was subsequently available.

The latter had physical holes, which allowed one to see a depiction of the constellation's stars when it was held up to a light!

TYPVS DE INTEGRO
Europa
MAGALLANICA
TERRA AUSTRALIS
PERUANA
MEXICANA

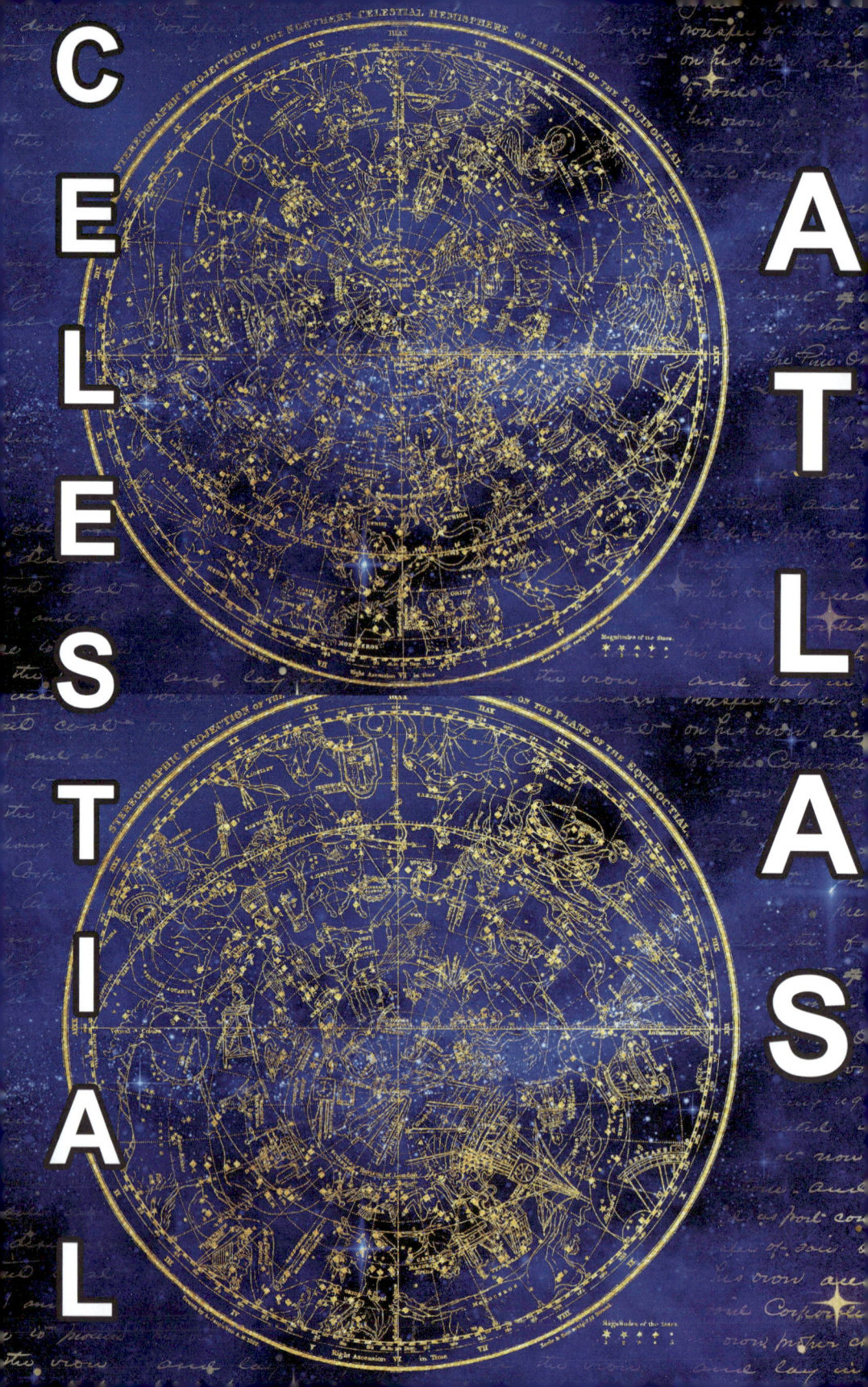

CELESTIAL ATLAS

MOON PHASES

RAM (AIRES) CONSTELLATION

BULL (TAURUS) CONSTELLATION

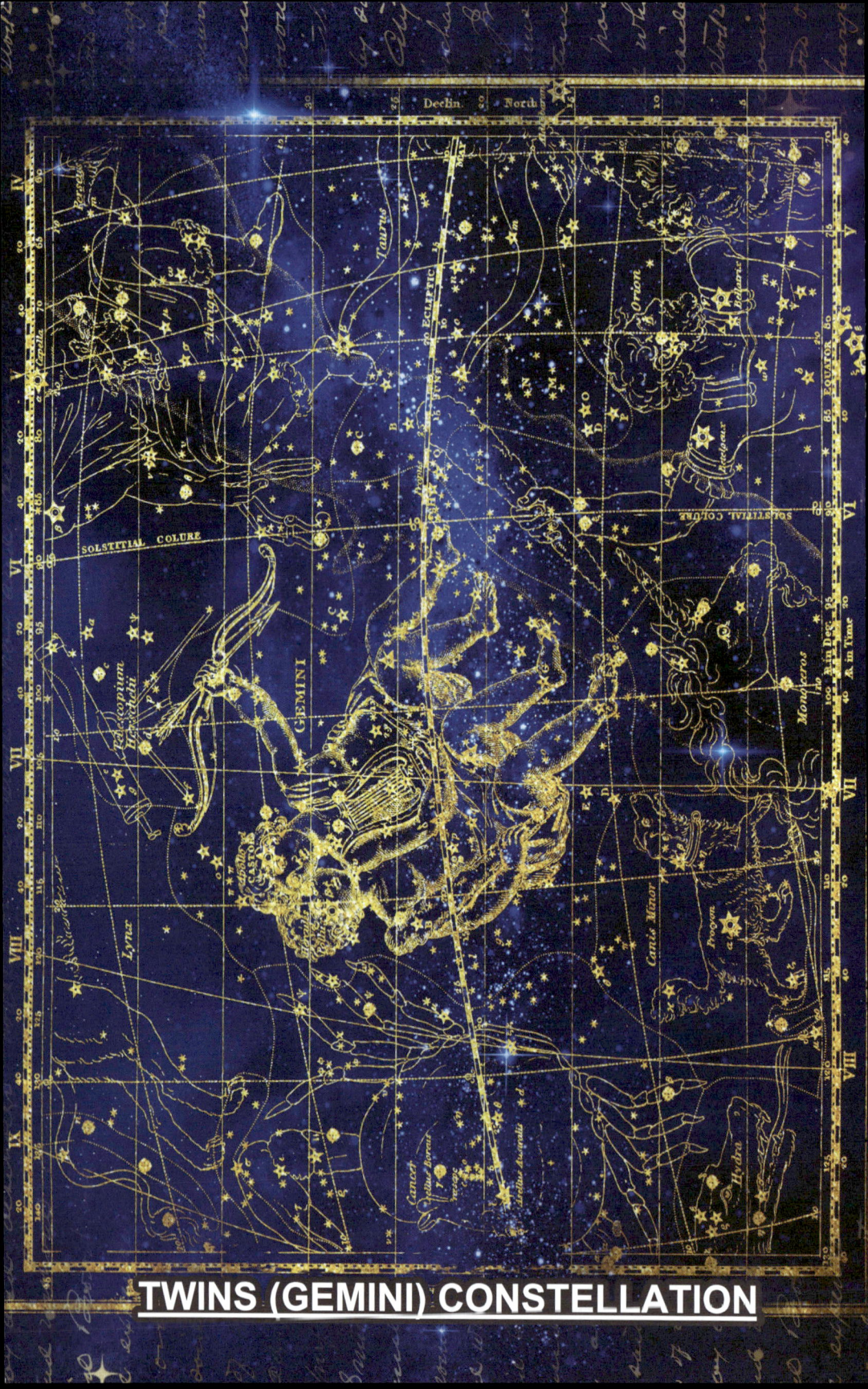

TWINS (GEMINI) CONSTELLATION

CRAB (CANCER) CONSTELLATION

LION (LEO) CONSTELLATION
"LEO THE LION"

* Together with "Hydra" and "Ursa Major", make up the three largest constellations visible in the night sky.

MAIDEN-VIRGIN (VIRGO) CONSTELLATION

**SCALES & SCORPION
(LIBRA - SCORPIO) CONSTELLATION**

CENTAUR (SAGATTORIUS) CONSTELLATION

**WATER BEARER & GOAT
(AQUARIUS & CAPRICORN)**

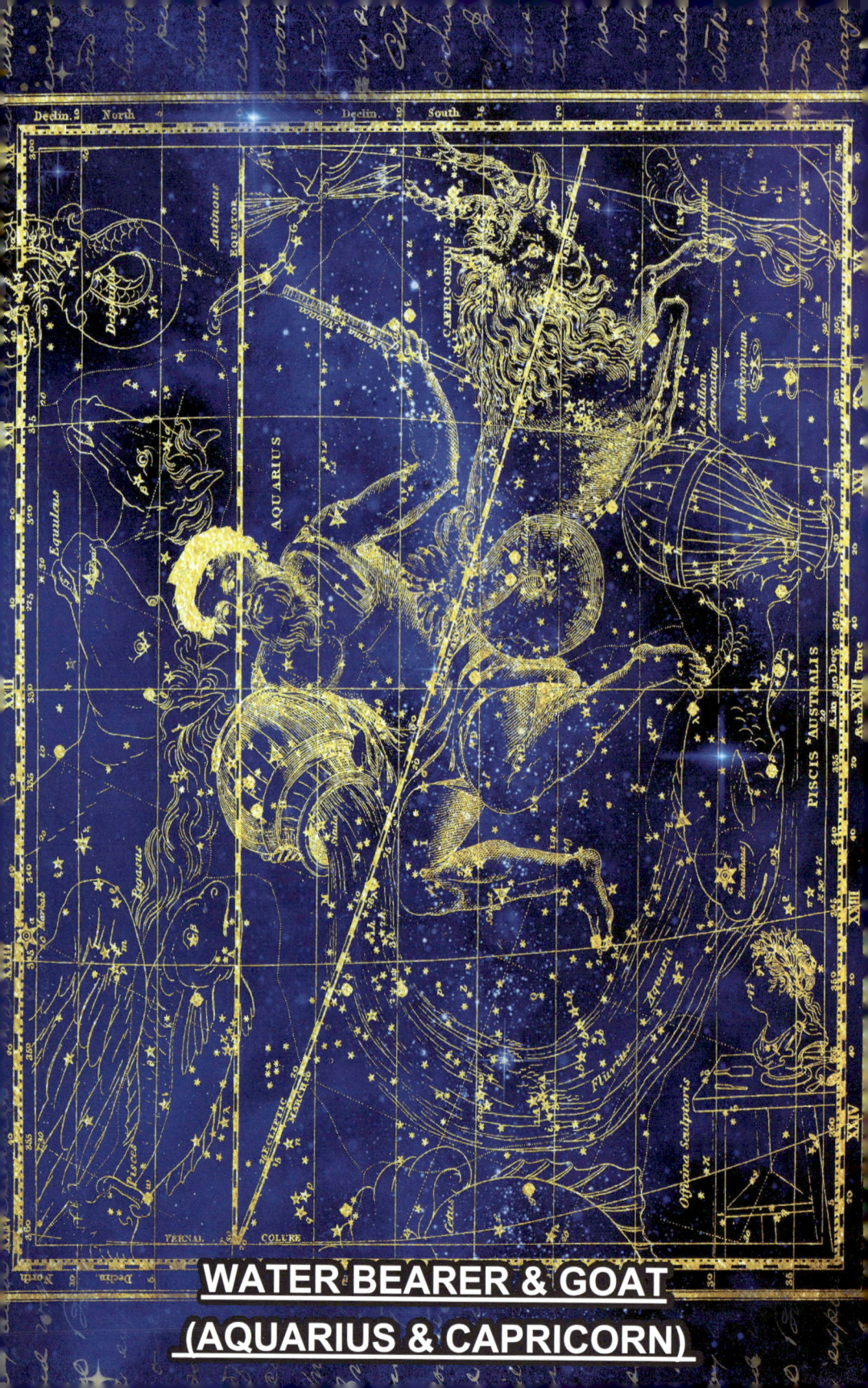

FISH (PISCES) CONSTELLATION

* The biggest of the 88 constellations. Its southern end abuts Libra, and Centaur at the northern end.

HYDRA (SEA SERPENT) CONSTELLATION

The third of the largest constellations in the night sky. "The Big Dipper", is made up of 7 bright stars in this complex.

URSA MAJOR (BIG BEAR) CONSTELLATION

PEGASUS CONSTELLATION

PEGASUS THE GREAT WHITE HORSE

"Pegasus" is one of the constellations in the Northern Sky. Like many others, Pegasus, like Ursa Major, their names are derived from Greek Mythology.

"Epsilon Pegasi", is the brightest star in its set, and makes up its muzzle.

"Alpha", "Beta", "Gamma"; and **"Alpha Andromedea"** (the largest star in the galaxy), form together its "Square", known as **"The Square of Pegasus"**.

Alpha Andromeda, like some other star systems, is actually a **binary** star system, with Alpha being the brighter visible star.

Other popular binary star systems include the following:
1. **"Sirius *A and B"** (Sirius A, being the brightest star in the visible night sky).
2. **"Epsilon Aurigae"**, and
3. **"Beta Lyrae"**.

"The Andromeda Galaxy", is the closest galaxy to Earth. It is a Spiral Galaxy, just like the galaxy system for Planet Earth, which is **"The Milky Way"**.

"Dear Reader,

Thank You for your interest in this book.

I hope it has inspired you, and you have found it enlightening."

* " I encourgae you to now pursue any new ideas you have had whilst reading !

I also encourage you to feel free to use this book to teach and inspire others, so that they too can grow.

With Love & Blessings.

- K C King "
09/04/2019

LIST OF REFERENCES:

A Vasques, M Doreal: The Emmerald Tablets of Thot the Atlantean, Plate 11. 30/07/1994

B Zuckerman: The occurrence of wide-orbit planets in binary star systems. The Astrophysical Journal Letters, 791:L27 (5pp). 20/08/2014. Website: https://iopscience.iop.org/article/10.1088/2041-8205/791/2/L27/pdf

Bernadine Fine Art and Jewellery: Gemstones Glossary: http://www.bernardine.com/gemstones/gemstones.htm

Cassandra Eason: Cassandra Eason's Illustrated Directory of Healing Crystals: An Illustrated Guide to 150 Crystals and Gemstones. 08/01/2015

D. I. Hoffman et al.: New β Lyrae and Algol candidates from the Northern Sky Variability Survey: The Astronomical Journal, 136:1067–1078. 09/2008 Website: https://iopscience.iop.org/article/10.1088/0004-6256/136/3/1067/pdf

Easteys Stuchiner: The 7 Chakras| What are they? : See Healing Institute. Website: https://selfhealinginstitute.com/7-chakras/

Eternal Ice Enterprises: Birthstones: http://eternal-ice.com/resources/birthstones/

F. Hammer et al.: The Astrophysical Journal, 662:322Y334. 10/07/2007. Website: https://iopscience.iop.org/article/10.1086/516727/pdf

Gal Einai: The Ten Sefirot - Introduction: http://www.inner.org/sefirot/sefirot.htm

Howard E Bond et al.: The Sirius System and Its Astrophysical Puzzles: Hubble Space Telescope and Ground-based Astrometry∗ :The Astrophysical Journal, 840:70 (17pp). 10/05/2017. Website: https://iopscience.iop.org/article/10.3847/1538-4357/aa6af8/pdf

Ian Ridpath, Alexander Jamieson.: Celestial map maker, Astronomy & Geophysics, Volume 54, Issue 1. 02/ 2013, p 1.22–1.23. Website: https://doi.org/10.1093/astrogeo/ats036

International Astronomical Society: Website: https://www.iau.org

IOPScience: https://iopscience.iop.org

Kosmic Energy Activation: Chakras: http://www.kea0.com/chakras/

M Parthasarathy, D Lambert.: Epsilon Aurigae in Eclipse. I. Ultraviolet Spectroscopy during Ingress and Totality: Publications of The Astronomical Society of the Pacific. 95:1012-1018. 12/1983. Website: https://iopscience.iop.org/article/10.1086/131283/pdf

LIST OF REFERENCES CONTINUED:

Patti Wigington: Birthstone Magic.: ThoughtCo. 26/09/2018. Website: https://www.thoughtco.com/about-birthstone-magic-4047863

Simon & Schuster: Guide to Gems and Precious Stones, 1986

The Awakened State: Numerology: https://theawakenedstate.net/numerology/

The Holy Bible: King James Version.

The Llewelyn Journal: The Angels of your Sun sign : Patricia Papps. 10/04/2017
Website: https://www.llewellyn.com/journal/article/2624

The Mystical Qablah: Dion Fortune. 31/08/2017

The Royal Astronomical Society: Website: https://ras.ac.uk

The Saturday Evening Post: "What Life Means to Einstein: An Interview by George Sylvester Viereck" : p 17, 110, 113, 114, 117. 26/10/1929

Walter Schumann: Gemstones of the World;Sterling Publishing Co., Inc.: Chalcedony, p 102,142, 284. 11/07/2013

Wikipedia: Astrological Sign : https://en.wikipedia.org/wiki/Astrological_sign

Wikipedia: Sefirot: https://en.wikipedia.org/wiki/Sefirot

Page left intentionally blank

FURTHER INTERESTING MATERIAL AND SUGGESTED READING:

Alexander Jamieson: A Celestial Atlas. Comprising A Systematic Display of the Heavens in a Series of Thirty Maps. 1822.

Bruce G. Knuth: Gems in Myth, Legend, and Lore: Jeweler's Press. 1999

Carlson R Chambliss: Eclipsing Binaries in Multiple Star Systems. Astronomical Society of the Pacific 104: 663-677. 08/1992

Colin Slater et al.: Andromeda XXVIII: A dwarf galaxy more than 350 kpc from Andromeda. The Astrophysical Journal Letters, 742:L14 (5pp). 20/11/ 2011

LearnKabbalah: Sechinah the Divine Feminine: https://learnkabbalah.com

Penny Billington, Ian Rees.: The keys to the Temple. 01/05/2017

Reverend Richard Rouse Bloxam: Urania's Mirror; or, a view of the Heavens. Teaching Aid Card Set. 1984

The Royal Astronomical Society: Treasures of the RAS: Urania's Mirror. Website: https://ras.ac.uk/library/treasures-of-the-ras/2428-treasures-of-the-ras-urania-s-mirror.

Page intentionally left blank

ATTRIBUTES WITH THANKS TO:

[1] Pixabay.com

For images licensed under Creative Commons 1.0 Universal (CC0 1.0) Public Domain.

Website: https://pixabay.com

[2] BookWright

The software provided by Blurb Books, that was used to create this book.

SPECIAL ATTRIBUTIONS TO THE FOLLOWING ARTISTS ON PIXABAY:

- Abstract Painted Face: *ivanovgood*
- Antique Celestial Planisphere Images: *DarkWorkX*
- Astrology, Chakra, Planetary Signs & Symbols: *Peter-Lomas, Openclipart-Vectors*
- Aum writing: *WikimediaImages 5818*
- Chakra & Mandalas on Bricks, Vintage Art: *Angela_Yuriko_Smith, CreatureSH*
- Hamsa, Ankh: *stux, TheDigitalArtist*
- Horoscope star constellations: *Gamol*
- Meditation Reflection: *Vivito Art*
- Metatrons cube: *NDV, socialtrendspr0, TheDigitalArtist*
- Mystical Doorway: *Kelepics*
- Mustard Seeds & shrubs: *gokalpiscan, Ajaypurva, Gertkeizjer, rihaij*
- Peace, writing: *Clker-Free-Vector-Images 29589, Bru-nO, bluebdugie*
- Precious stones : *Didgeman, RobertR, eminens, annca, PaulaPaulsen, ImageParty, rikkerst, gracielazerpaurbina, klaber, sarakgraves, Fotocitizen, caro_eo92*
- Trees, Forests: *jplenio, O12*
- Tutankhamun Bust : *Sriom*
- Quill: *LunarSeaArt226, Sponchia*
- Zodiac signs: *geralt, Sarah_Loetcher, _vane_, kidaha, Trandoshan*

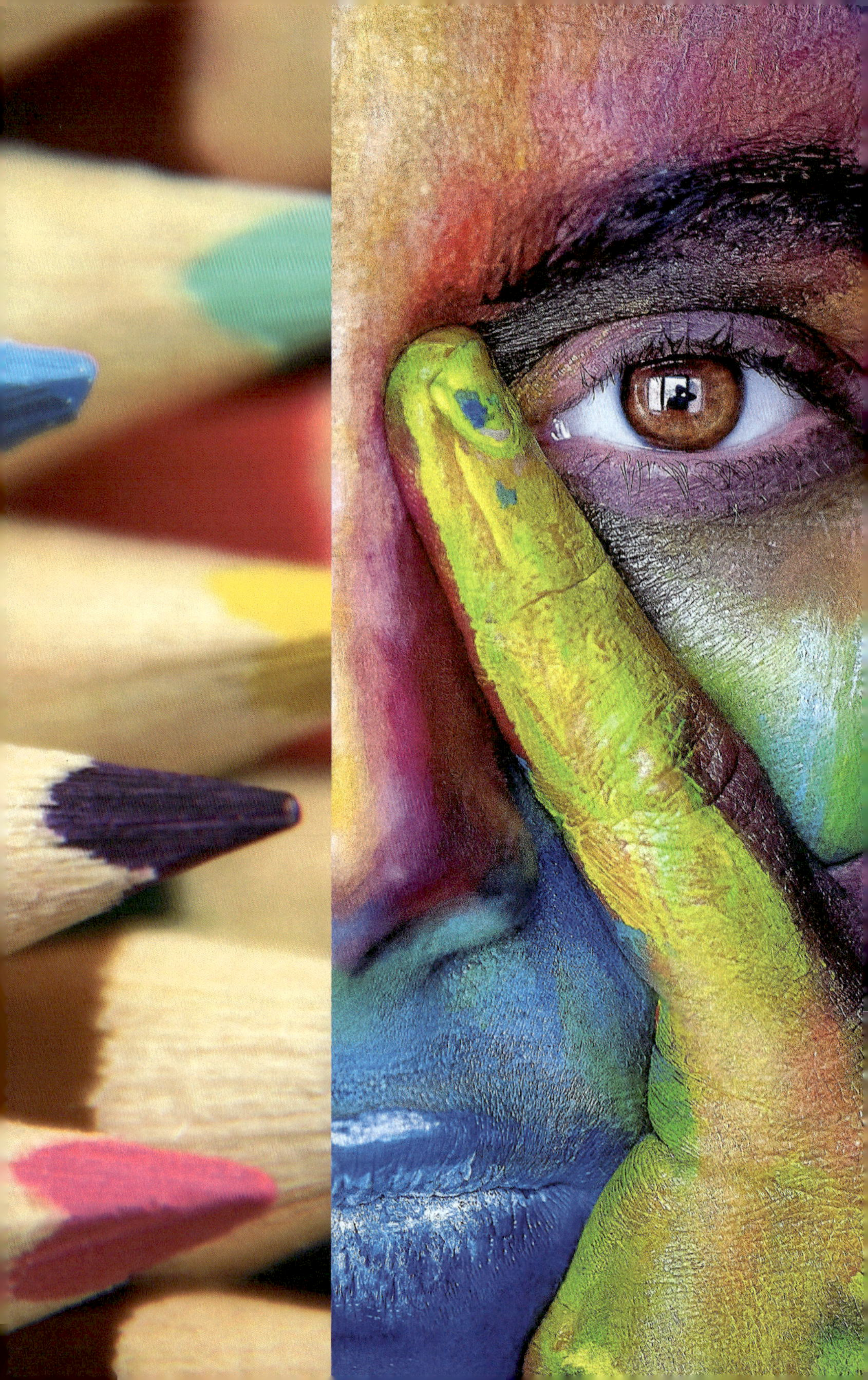

*"Each has his own part to
play in the cycles.
Each has his work to
complete in his way.
The cycle below thee is yet
not below thee
but only formed for a need
that exists.
For know ye that the
fountain of wisdom
that sends forth the cycles is
eternally
seeking new powers to gain.
Ye know that knowledge is
gained only by practice,
and wisdom comes forth
only from knowledge,
and thus are the cycles
created by Law.
Means are they for the
gaining of knowledge
for the Plane of Law that is
the Source of the All. "*

**- The Emerald Tablets of
Thoth the Atlantean,
Tablet 11**

ABOUT THE AUTHOR

I was born in the Republic of Trinidad & Tobago. I have been blessed to live in a variety of countries, having gained exposure to various religio-cultural systems. These experiences have broadened my perspective on life.

This book is also a work book on reflections, for life can be viewed like a series of reflections. This book reflects all thoughts above, through my love and appreciation for religion, colour and art.

I view "Creation" as a masterpiece and work of art, wherein each soul has their own canvas to paint. I encourage you to go forth, and be your own artist!

- Krystal C KING 04/2019

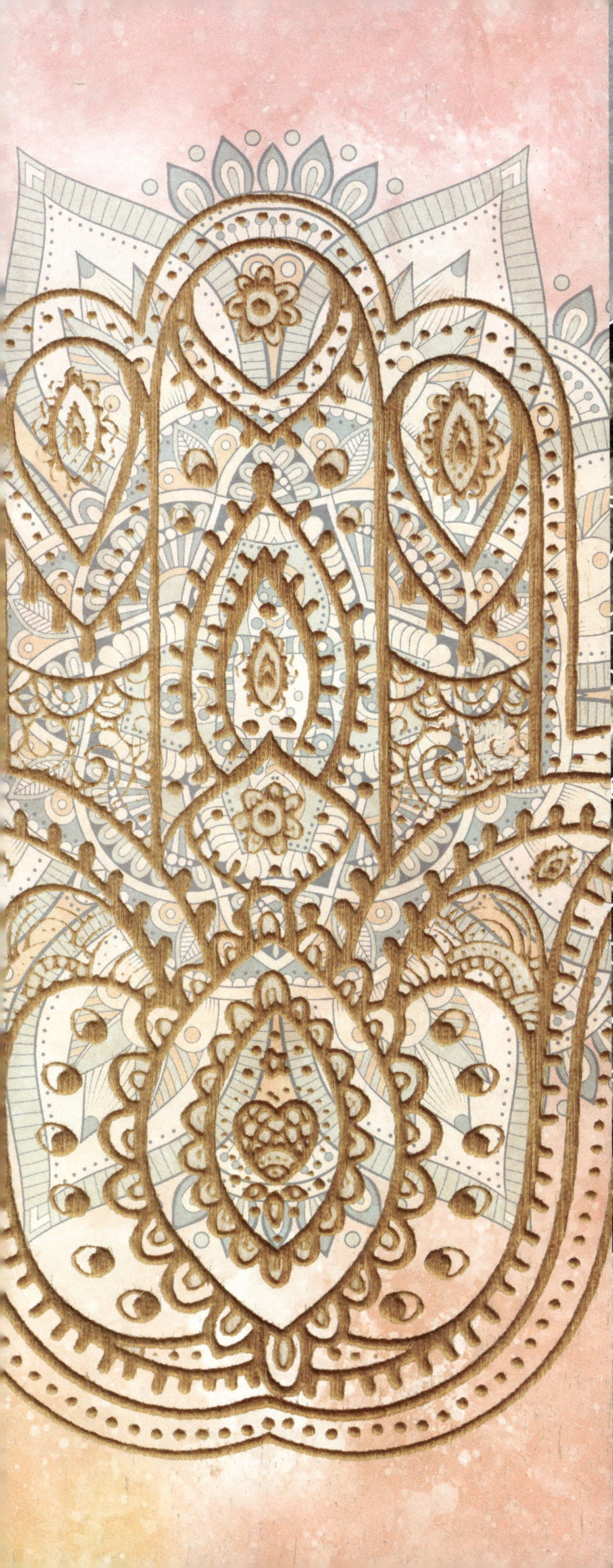
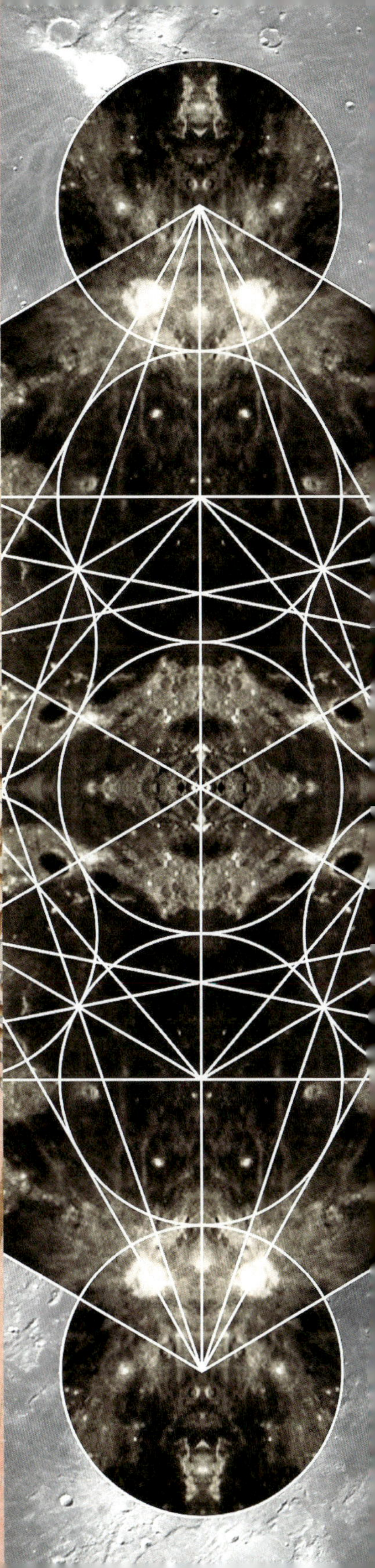

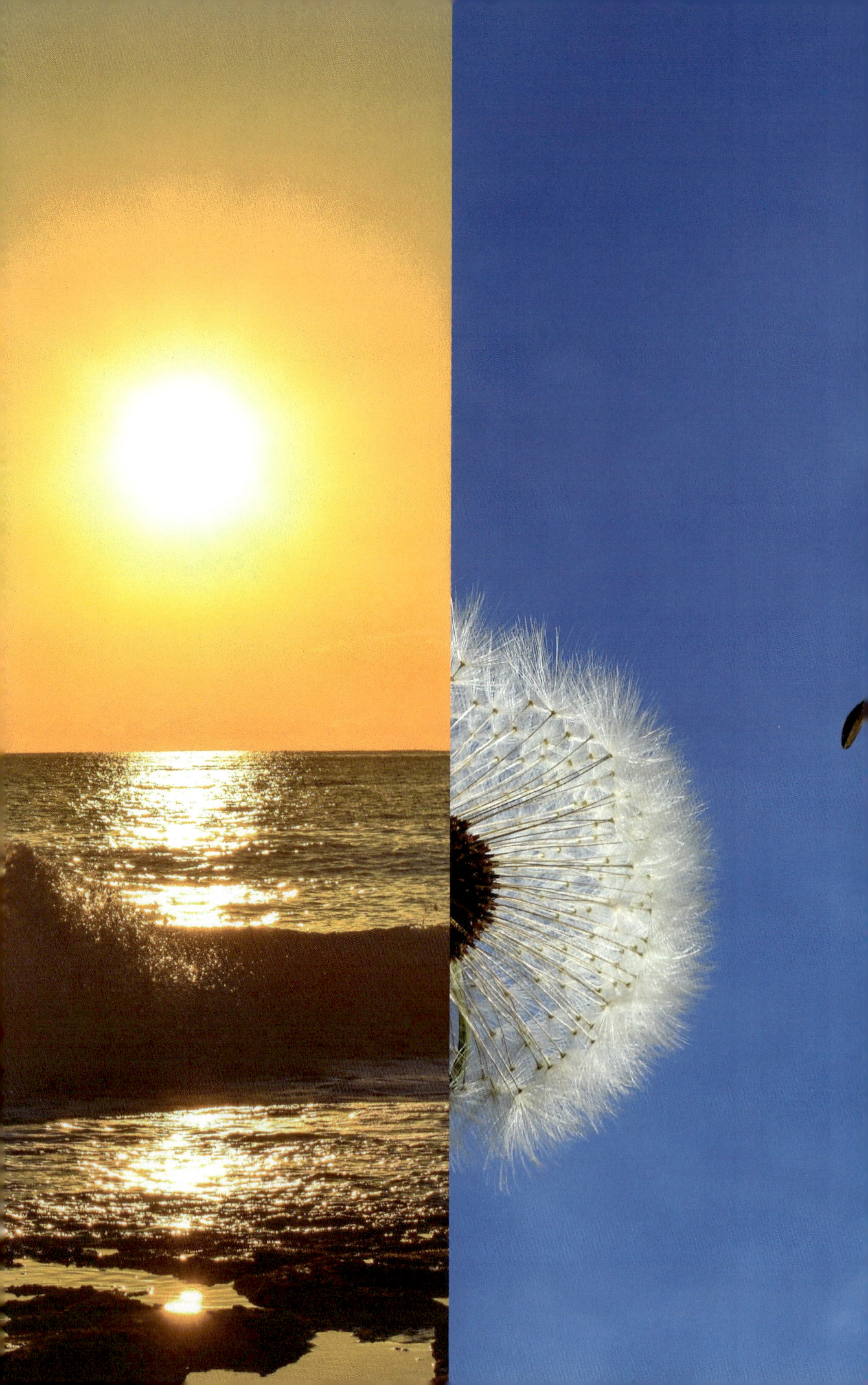

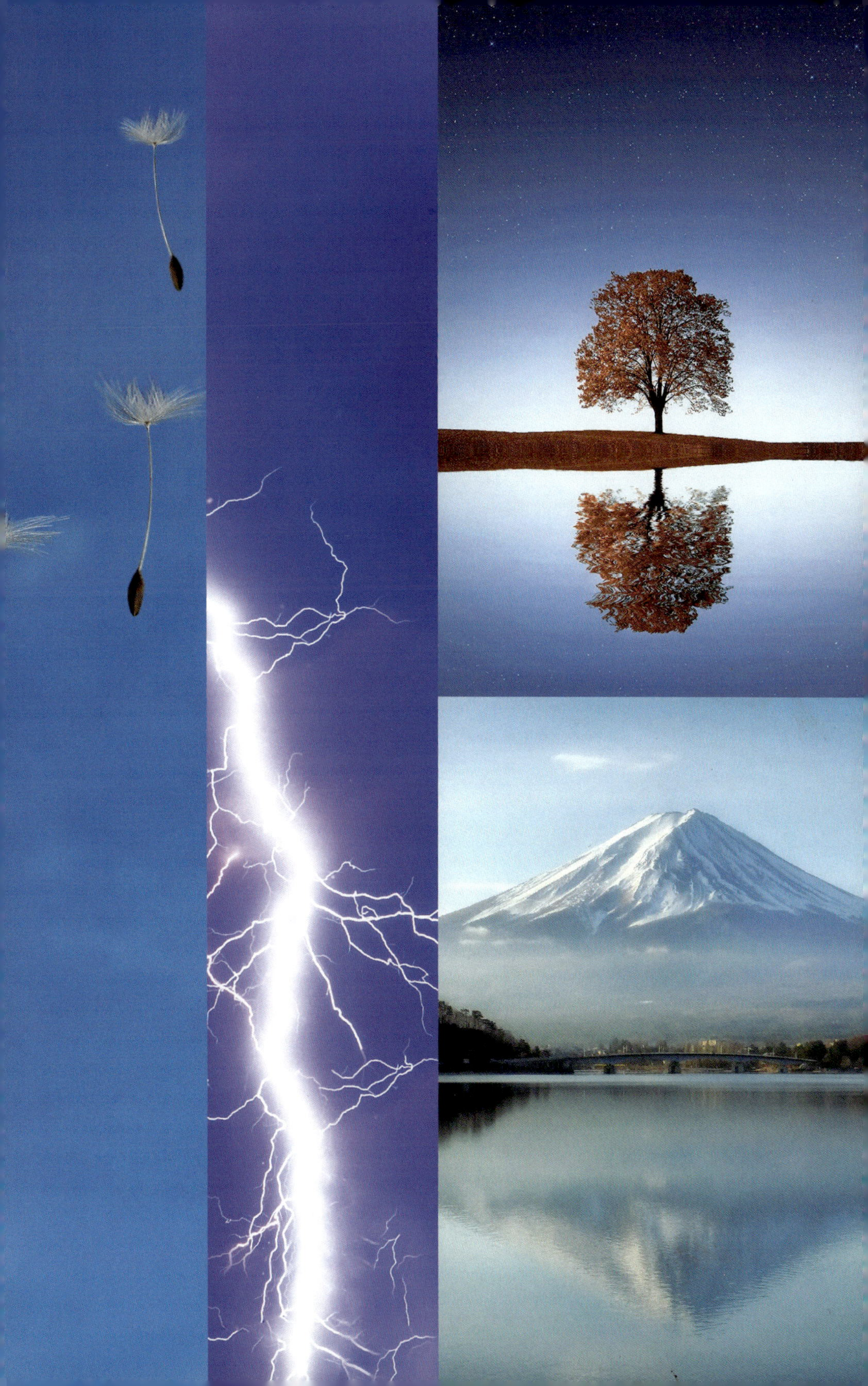

* You can use these following pages to start to visualise and plan your ideas: